THE
SOUTHERN
UPLAND
WAY

Also available
The Cotswold Way
The Dales Way
The Saxon Shore Way
The West Highland Way
The Two Moors Way

RECREATIONAL PATH GUIDE

THE
SOUTHERN
UPLAND WAY

ANTHONY BURTON

Photographs by Rob Scott

Aurum Press

Ordnance
Survey

First published in Great Britain 1997
by Aurum Press Ltd, 25 Bedford Avenue, London WC1B 3AT
in association with the Ordnance Survey.

A catalogue record for this book is available
from the British Library.

ISBN 1 85410 455 1

2 4 6 8 10 9 7 5 3 1
1998 2000 2001 1999 1997

Designed by Robert Updegraff
Printed and bound in Italy by Printers Srl Trento

Cover: *The Southern Upland Way heading towards the hills, north of
St John's Town of Dalry.*
Title page: *Footbridge over a bustling stream on the approach to
Watch Water Reservoir.*

CONTENTS

How to use this guide   6
Distance checklist   7
Keymaps   8

Introduction
Walking the Southern Upland Way   13
The Southern Uplands Landscape   17
The Troubled Border   19
Wildlife   23
Lead Mining   26
Castles and Abbeys   27
Sir Walter Scott   30

The Southern Upland Way

1 Portpatrick to Castle Kennedy   36

2 Castle Kennedy to Bargrennan   44

3 Bargrennan to St John's Town of Dalry   58

4 St John's Town of Dalry to Sanquhar   74

5 Sanquhar to Wanlockhead   90

6 Wanlockhead to Beattock   96

7 Beattock to St Mary's Loch   106

8 St Mary's Loch to Traquair   118

9 Traquair to Melrose   126

10 Melrose to Longformacus   140

11 Longformacus to Cockburnspath   152

Useful Information
Transport   164
Accommodation   164
Tourist Information Centres   165
Useful addresses   166
Southern Upland Way Countryside Rangers   166
Ordnance Survey maps covering the Southern Upland Way 167
Bibliography   167
Places to visit on or near the Southern Upland Way   167

How to use this guide

This guide is in three parts:
• The introduction, historical background to the area and advice for walkers.
• The path itself, described in eleven chapters, with maps opposite each route description. This part of the guide also includes information on places of interest. Key sites are numbered in the text and on the maps to make it easy to follow the route description.
• The last part includes useful information such as local transport, accommodation, organizations involved with the path, and further reading.

The maps have been prepared by Ordnance Survey® for this guide using 1:25 000 Pathfinder® maps as a base. In Scotland rights of way are not marked on Ordnance Survey maps, as is the case south of the border. The only established rights of way are those where a court case has resulted in a legal settlement, but there are thousands of other 'claimed' rights of way. Many paths and tracks were built by estates as stalking paths or for private paths or for private access, therefore a path on a map is no indication of right of way. While using such paths you should follow the Country Code, taking care to avoid damage to property and the natural environment. The line of the Southern Upland Way is shown in yellow. Any parts of the path that may be difficult to follow on the ground are clearly highlighted in the route description, and important points to watch out for are marked with letters in each chapter, both in the text and in the maps. *Some maps start on a right-hand page and continue on a left-hand page – black arrows (➜) at the edge of the maps indicate the start point.* Should there have been a need to alter the route since publication of this guide for any reason, walkers are advised to follow the waymarks or signs that have been put on the site to indicate this.

DISTANCE CHECKLIST

This list will help you in calculating the distances between places on the Southern Upland Way, whether you are planning your overnight stays or checking your progress.

Location	Approximate distance from previous location	
	miles	*km*
Portpatrick	0	0
Castle Kennedy	13.5	21.5
New Luce	9.5	15
Bargrennan	17.5	28
St John's Town of Dalry	27.5	36
Sanquhar	25	40
Wanlockhead	8	13
Beattock	20	32
St Mary's Loch	21	33
Traquair	12	19
Galashiels	13	20
Lauder	13.5	21.5
Longformacus	15	24.5
Cockburnspath	18	29

INTRODUCTION

The Southern Upland Way climbs up from the Tweed Valley to wind across Hog Hill towards Galashiels.

WALKING THE SOUTHERN UPLAND WAY

The first point may seem obvious, but does still need to be stressed: this is a very long walk and those who set off to walk the whole Way in one go need to be sure they have the stamina and fitness to achieve their ambition. It is not only a long walk, but can also be a very demanding one, for there are lengthy moorland sections that offer little if anything in the way of protection. It is usual to walk the route from west to east – the description that follows is based on that premise – mainly because the prevailing winds are westerly. This does not mean that warm westerly winds are guaranteed: I, when walking the route in May to make notes for this book, was faced with north-easterlies nearly all the way across and suffered the decidedly uncomfortable experience of walking head-on into a hailstorm at the very top of the very bleakest moor. So, the next and most obvious advice is, prepare for the worst. Always ensure that you are properly shod – good walking boots really are the best answer – and have waterproof and windproof clothing.

The route description has been broken down into sections for convenient reference, but you should not assume that these are the legs that you have to walk. In practice, the length of a day's walk will be largely determined by availability of accommodation. Those who carry their own tents will obviously have the greatest flexibility, and they can supplement camping out with occasional nights in bothies. For others, a glance at the map will show that there are very few towns and villages actually on the Way. The situation, however, is not as bad as it seems, for there are a number of isolated bed and breakfast houses *en route*. Even so, they are thin on the ground and it is advisable to book well in advance. Those who are still unsure about managing some of the longest legs still need not despair. Many bed and breakfast owners are happy to arrange meetings along the way and will take you back to the same spot to start again the next day. An even easier alternative is to use an organization such as Make Tracks, which will not only arrange accommodation, fix pick-up and set-down points, but – ultimate luxury – will arrange for your back pack or luggage to be moved while you walk along with just a day pack. There is one other possibility to consider if you are nervous about the sheer length of the walk: it is possible to split it into two parts by using Sanquhar, with its good rail connections, as the break point.

All the normal rules for long-distance walking apply. Even those who are taking just a day pack should make sure they have a full range of weatherproof clothing, essential first aid, torch, whistle and enough food and drink – for there is often nowhere to stop and buy anything for the whole of a day's walk. This guide contains detailed maps and instructions for finding your route, and the waymarking is excellent throughout. Posts marked with a this-tle in a hexagon indicate you are going the right way, and yellow arrows are added to show changes in direction. But even this alone is not enough. This is indeed an *upland* way, and clouds can come down over the hills very quickly, reducing visibility quite alarmingly. In such cases suggested landmarks and direction posts can disappear and your only reliable guides are map and compass. So be very sure that you know how to use a compass before you set off. The top of a mountain in driving rain is not the place for a first experiment. The Southern Upland Way also has its own peculiarities. A good deal of the route goes through and by forest. The Ordnance Survey maps show these areas very clearly, but they cannot show what you will find on the ground. You might be expecting a great area of tall conifers and panic when nothing like it appears anywhere in view. It is only when you reach the area that you might find it is a new plantation with the trees still only a few inches high and scarcely visible from a distance, or that it was indeed an area of tall trees, but now they have been felled. Tree felling, of course, goes on all the time, sometimes along the line of the Way. When that happens, diversions have to be taken. These will be clearly marked, and may lengthen the walk, though probably not by very much, and, more importantly, they may take you over far rougher ground than you expected. As one walker ruefully noted at the end of such a section: 'that wasn't a diver-sion: it was an assault course'. The other problem that may occur is on the grouse moors. Walkers are asked to be especially careful to keep to the Way during the nesting season in April and May, and there may be diversions when the guns are out on the moor during the shooting season that starts on 12 August.

Twisted roots of dead trees beside Clatteringshaws Loch, and the living conifers that surround it can be seen in the distance.

Sheep thrive on the rich pasture at Blackburn Mill on Eye Water near the eastern end of the Way.

Two other questions need to be answered at the planning stage: when to walk and how long to allow for the journey. The most popular time for walking the Way is late spring and early summer: the winter snows have, with luck, retreated and the dreaded Scots insects, midges and flies, have not yet appeared, and there is the added advantage of long days. But each season has its virtues. Late summer and autumn offer the glories of heather in bloom, while winter is magnificent for those who come equipped and prepared to meet the challenge. As to how long to plan for the whole walk, the answer must depend on the individual's capabilities and fitness. Two weeks is generally recognized as a happy choice, which allows a good deal of flexibility, perhaps slipping in a half-day after a couple of days' hard going. The golden rule is overestimate rather than underestimate. It is far better to have time to spare than to end the day in a state of miserable near exhaustion.

Finally there are two myths to dispel about this route. The first is that you will spend all your time walking through conifer forests. This is, quite simply, not true. Along the way you will find everything from strolls through gentle farmland to some of the finest open-moorland walking that Britain can offer. True, there is a good deal of forestation, but even that has a great deal of variety to offer. The second is that, quite inexplicably, many people seem to think that an immense amount of road walking is involved. Quite simply, there is no more road walking on this route than you would expect to find on any long-distance path. At the end of this walk, the overwhelming memories of the Southern Upland Way are of immense solitudes with only birdsong for company, and of standing by lonely cairns, staring out over mile upon mile of glorious rolling hills. If ever there was a walk for those who, in the old hackneyed phrase, 'want to get away from it all', this is it.

THE SOUTHERN UPLANDS LANDSCAPE

The name 'Southern Uplands' is not a term devised to provide a popular name for a long-distance walk, but describes a very distinct geological region. Anyone who has walked the West Highland Way will have become aware of the dramatic change of scenery that occurs where the Highland Boundary Fault appears near the southern end of Loch Lomond. To the south of that is the Midland Valley or Central Lowlands, which ends at another, if not quite so spectacular feature, the Southern Upland Fault. This marks the northern edge of the country through which walkers make their way.

Here is an area of very ancient rocks, formed during the Lower Palaeozoic period around 500 million years ago. We think of rocks as the epitome of stability, but when these were new their home was south of the equator, and they were making a slow journey northwards. What we now know as England and Scotland were separate masses separated by sea, and when they finally collided the sediments on the sea bed were pushed up to form hills. You can see this sedimentary rock most clearly at the start of the walk, the greywacke, a form of sandstone, in the cliffs around Portpatrick. Inland, the hills were gradually eroded, then crushed down and smoothed out by the Ice Ages that began around a million and a half years ago and only ended a mere 10,000 years ago – a very modern event in the context of geological time. Rounded hills and glaciated valleys characterize

The little stream at Potburn that will soon grow into a river as it flows down the Eltrick Water valley.

most of the walk, while material washed down by erosion flattened out to create valley floors.

This, in very brief outline, explains the overall pattern of the landscape, but the detail owes as much to man's intervention as to nature – though nature has had the last word on how man uses the land. To the west of the region, hard granite has pushed up through the softer sedimentary rocks to create an altogether more rugged landscape than that of the east. The rains generally driven by westerly winds ensure that this is a decidedly damp region, in which peat bogs are commonplace. Once it was heavily forested, but this was not a region that encouraged the growing of crops, so hardy cattle and sheep were set out to graze. The land was gradually cleared, and the steadily munching flocks and herds kept it that way. It is only in recent years that the forests have returned: not the native species but close-packed plantations of mainly North American spruce and pine.

The fault line is not the only natural boundary. The River Nith, which flows through Sanquhar is another. To the east of it, the land is generally drier, the granite intrusions disappear and the hills are altogether smoother and more rounded. Grass and heather provide good grazing, and down in the valleys the richer soil makes arable farming possible. Here, larger towns such as Galashiels developed, based on a thriving woollen industry. The new mills of the towns, developed mainly in the 19th century, pulled in families from the surrounding villages and hamlets, many of which declined or disappeared completely. Grazing land was turned into grouse moors for the rich. So the walker will find a thinly populated country, with wide vistas over rolling hills that seem timeless, but which are the product of a process of continuous change.

THE TROUBLED BORDER

The border that wriggles its way from the Solway Firth to the Tweed is, in historical terms, something of a newcomer. There was nothing that could be called a border at all until the Emperor Hadrian visited Britain in AD 121 and ordered a wall to be built to separate Roman Britain from the war-like tribes of the north. Twenty years later the frontier moved north with the construction of the Antonine Wall from the Forth to the Clyde. That was a short-lived venture, and the Romans retreated back to the safety of Hadrian's defences. A rough division had been established between southern and northern Britain, but the nation of Scotland had still to be established. The Scots were in fact one of just four powerful groups in the region. The first were the Celts from Ireland, who disputed the northern part of the area with the Picts. Further south were the other Celtic groups, the Britons, and Anglo-Saxons from the Rhineland and the Baltic. It was not until 843 that Kenneth MacAlpine overcame the Picts to become King of the Scots, but he was unable to overcome the Angles to the south. Finally, in 1018 Scotland became one country.

The area through which the Southern Upland Way passes was thus very much a border region. To the north were the Celts, speaking a different language and retaining the tribal identity of the clans; to the south were the English in what was soon to become a Norman kingdom. Raiders or reivers went north and south attacking small communities and carrying back cattle and goods, and reivers from south and north returned the compliment. It was not an area in which to enjoy a guaranteed peaceful existence. Above and beyond these local skirmishes were greater national rivalries, which produced conflict and, on occasions, wars. There are remains of these times along the Way.

Edward I successfully invaded Scotland and declared himself king in 1296. Opposition soon appeared. It was first led by William Wallace, who defeated Edward's forces at Stirling Bridge and in 1297 was declared Warden of Scotland. The ceremony is said to have taken place in a little chapel, of which only the grave-yard remains, by St Mary's Loch. The pendulum swung again as Wallace was defeated the following year. The next revolt against the English was led by Robert the Bruce. He too was defeated and forced to flee, and it was in this period that, famously, he gained inspiration from a spider in a cave and regrouped his forces. The confident English under the Earl of Pembroke set off to finish the job of quelling rebellion. Walkers following the Way along the southern shore of Loch Trool are following the path taken by Pembroke's troops. As they passed below the steep slopes of Mulldonnoch, an avalanche of boulders descended on them followed by Bruce's men. They were completely routed and the fortunes of war were changed. Following the victory at Bannockburn in 1314, Scotland was independent again.

This did not mean an end to troubles in the Border region. Clans still fought among themselves. The Waverley Castle Hotel near Galashiels stands on Skirmish Hill, where the last clan battle was fought in the area in 1526. But most of the trouble came inevitably from conflict with the authorities in England. But of all

Polgown Farm near Sanquhar is typical of the region, with its sparkling whitewashed walls and row of dormer windows.

The Pease Deane nature reserve near Cockburnspath has been planted with native trees to encourage the development of varied flora and fauna.

the troubles that beset the southern Scots few were as vicious as those that became known as the 'killing time'. The trouble began when Charles I attempted to force a version of the English Prayer book on the Scottish Presbyterians. In 1638 the Lowland Scots responded by publishing a National Covenant setting out their own beliefs. It was as much a declaration of the Scots' right to determine their own affairs as a theological document. Events overtook the quarrel as the Civil War began. Now Parliament looked to Scottish support and offered a new League and Covenant, guaranteeing them religious freedom. At the Restoration trouble broke out again. Charles II tried to reverse the reforms, and those Covenanters who refused to return to the old ways were once again in revolt against the king in England. At the Market Cross in Sanquhar, Richard Cameron called for armed insurrection and the fate of the Covenanters was sealed. Men who wanted no more than to practise their religion among their parishioners were outlawed and put to death in the 'killing time' of the 1680s. The Martyr's Memorial in Glen Trool is a poignant reminder of those days.

The Jacobite Rebellion affected the Highlands far more than the Lowlands and when that was ended, this troubled region at last knew peace.

WILDLIFE

The walk begins and ends among the raucous clamour of sea birds. As well as the familiar gulls, the cliffs around Portpatrick are home to colonies of fulmars and gannets. The former are among the great gliders of the bird world, seeming to keep effortlessly aloft on stiff wings, while the latter are noted for their spectacular dives into the sea. Gannets have been recorded as hitting the water at speeds of 100km an hour. Pease Bay at the opposite end of the walk offers a chance to see that other great fisher, the cormorant, waiting patiently on a rock before plunging into the water.

Along the Way, the bird life varies with the terrain, and the season. In open terrain, the smaller birds may sometimes appear slightly drab, but compensate with their songs. In spring and early summer, meadow pippets seem to find singing hard work as they climb, but achieve full melodic beauty as they descend gently to the ground, while the skylark's beautiful song has cheered many a solitary walker. The wheatear is rather more colourful than the

A farm house takes advantage of the shelter of trees and a gully on the Way between St Mary's Loch and Traquair.

others, but rarely does more than utter a hard clacking call, though it too is capable of beautiful notes when in flight. The golden plover is heard at its best in the spring, when it soars to great heights. But of all the bird calls heard along the way, none is more evocative of the lonely moorland than the plaintive cry that gives the bird its name – curlew. In winter the snow bunting is one of the few remaining songbirds. One of the less common species that may be heard as well as seen is the ring ouzel, a mountain-dwelling member of the blackbird family, distinguished by its white collar.

Birds of prey are regularly seen on the uplands and while kestrels are the most common, buzzards, hen harriers, merlins and peregrines may all be encountered. One bird is likely to see you before you see it and act immediately. You can get quite close to a red grouse on the ground before it suddenly flies up with a violent whirr of feathers. Some of the moors are used to rear grouse for shooting, and walkers should beware of shooting parties anytime between 12 August and 10 December.

The woodland areas offer a home to other species, which might be seen in the sparse areas given over to broad-leaved trees, but are more likely simply to be heard in the denser conifer plantations. Among the more interesting inhabitants are the Scottish crossbill – a species in its own right – and the agile little siskin, often seen hanging onto seemingly impossible thin twigs. Short-eared owls are not uncommon, but are more rarely seen.

Pride of place among the animal life has to go to the deer. Both red deer and roe deer are found along the Way and there is a good deal of information about these beautiful creatures at the Clatteringshaws Forest Wildlife Centre on the west shore of Clatteringshaws Loch. Among the other woodland inhabitants are herds of wild goats – which are often detected by their distinctly powerful smell before they are seen. Some walkers may be fortunate enough to catch a glimpse of a mountain hare in the Lowther Hills. English visitors will also enjoy the chance to see the red squirrel, now a rarity further south. A rather less welcome sight is the adder, which is dangerous, but will do its best to keep away from humans, who should be equally keen to keep away from it. There is an abundance of wildlife all along the Southern Upland Way and walkers will find that taking a pair of binoculars will greatly add to their enjoyment of it.

LEAD MINING

Walkers on the Southern Upland Way could be forgiven for thinking that the last thing they would come across would be the
extensive remains of an industry that lasted in the region for
nearly two thousand years. Yet that is exactly what will be found
in the area around Wanlockhead. No one can be certain when
mining first began here, but the Romans were certainly busy and
found extensive deposits of lead, and enough gold and silver to
earn the area its popular name of 'God's Treasure House in
Scotland'.

As happened in so many parts of Britain, mining activity came
to a halt once the Romans left, and large-scale activity only recom-
menced in the 16th century when the Elizabethan adventurer Sir
Bevis Bulmer came up to the region to try his luck. He was followed by the Hope family, who established a village for the miners, which they modestly called Hopetown, and when they made
their fortune they became Earls of Hopetown. The name, however,
did not last, and Hopetown became mundane Leadhills. By the
18th century Leadhills and Wanlockhead were booming, and
even featured as places to be visited by the more inquisitive
tourists of the day. Robert Heron wrote an account of a tour of the
West of Scotland in 1792 and described the area as 'bleak, wild
and lofty', a description the modern walker would not dispute.
What he also found was a desperately hard-working community.
'The labour of the miner is severe and unremitting. Through night
and day it is continued.' Because of the remoteness of the area,
the miners had to fend for themselves, returning at the end of the
shift to work their little kitchen gardens. Heron commended the
community for its virtuous nature, which was not, in his view, a
reflection of the good character of the local people, but entirely
due to the sound thinking of the owners, who worked the miners
so hard that they had no energy left for sinning. Even he, however,
was impressed by the fact that the people of both villages had
libraries. The earlier one at Leadhills, begun in 1741 by the poet
Allan Ramsay, was the first public subscription library in Britain.

The mines continued to prosper in the 19th century and received
a great boost when a London company, the Leadhills Silver-Lead
Mining & Smelting Company re-equipped the mines and rebuilt
most of the village of Leadhills. The industry was sufficiently important at the end of the century for the Caledonian Railway to build a
light railway from their main line up to Wanlockhead, which then

boasted the highest summit of any railway – apart from specialist mountain railways – in Britain. But the industry went into decline, the railway was closed after less than four decades of use in 1938 and the buildings and structures of a once great industry began slowly to crumble – but not actually to disappear.

The extensive remains have now been preserved as part of the Museum of Lead Mining. The old shafts and spoil heaps, smelters and tramways along which horses drew the trucks of ore and the complex system of waterways used to power water wheels and wash the ore can all still be seen. The local mines suffered from a problem common to all deep mines, water, which had to be pumped out. One answer was the steam engine, and among those who came to build pumping engines was William Symington, one of the pioneers of steam boats, whose first little steamer was given a trial on a lake near Dumfries, with Robert Burns among the passengers. But the most interesting survivor is not a steam pump but a water-powered beam pump. This is a most curious device. Water fills a bucket, which eventually drops down, and as it does so it hauls up the pump rods suspended from the opposite end of an overhead beam. At the bottom of its fall, the bucket hits a catch that releases the water. Then the bucket shoots up again, the pump rods plunge and the whole cycle restarts. Thanks to the ever-nodding beam, men could work far underground fetching up the ore on which two communities depended for their livelihood. For those who can make time for exploration along the Way, Wanlockhead is an area well worth discovering.

CASTLES AND ABBEYS

Given the troubled history of the Border region it is no surprise to find fortifications of various kinds dotted along the route, but the earliest date back to a time before the border itself existed. In the Iron Age, which lasted from around 500 BC to *c.* AD 50, Britain was occupied by a multitude of tribal groups each defending its own vaguely defined territory. At the heart of such a group would be a fort, typically built on top of a hill, with the natural defences improved on by ditches and ramparts circling the summit. Beattock hill fort is a small but typical example, though the effect is some-what marred by the use of part of the site as a council rubbish tip. A more impressive example can be seen overlooking Whiteadder Water, south of Abbey St Bathans. Edin's Hall, legendary home of the giant Edin, began with a fort with double ramparts and ditches, but then, at the end of the Iron Age, a far more impressive fortress was added. This was a broch, a circular tower with double walls, with rooms set within the cavity. Its walls are 5 metres thick and still stand to a height of 1.5 metres. It has three sets of rooms with guard rooms flanking the entrance.

Most of the castles met along the Way were begun in the medieval period; they may, however, have been much changed over the years. And none has seen more alterations than the grandest of them all, Traquair House, which claims to be the oldest continuously occupied house in Scotland. Alexander I visited here in 1107, but what he saw would have borne no resemblance to what we see today. The old wooden building of his day was later torn down and a stone tower erected in its place, which in turn became the centre of a very grand, if still stern, house. There was a major rebuilding in the 17th century in suitably baronial style. Legend has it that the famous ornate gates are to remain closed until the Stuarts return to the throne. Happily, the same fate has not overtaken the 18th-century brewhouse, which was reopened and produces an excellent beer that can be sampled in local pubs. Thirlestane Castle is also still inhabited. There was a fort here in the 13th century, while the massive turreted keep was added in 1590. Over the years it was gradually extended, culminating in a major rebuild in the 1840s. The other castles are more or less ruined. Sanquhar was begun in the 14th century, but abandoned 300 years later. Castle Kennedy had an even shorter history. Built by the Kennedys in 1607 it was accidentally burned down in 1716 and never rebuilt. But its grounds were landscaped and the splendid formal gardens can still be seen. Perhaps the most typical of border fortresses are the single towers, with no hint of domesticity about them. They are survivors from the age of the reivers, raiding and plundering on both sides of the border. Blackhouse Tower is one of the oldest, but nearby Dryhope Tower is better preserved. This is a 16th-century peel tower, not meant as a permanent home but as a place to retreat to when the raiders came.

Peaceful religious communities did survive the brutalities and bloodshed of medieval life, and have left behind buildings of great beauty. Glenluce Abbey, seen in the distance from the Way, looks somewhat unimpressive. It is only close to that its glories can be appreciated. Founded by the Cistercians in 1190, not much of the church remains, but the delightful little chapter house has sur-

Traquair House has been domesticated but still shows something of the stern grandeur of its origins as a medieval castle.

vived with its traceried windows, stone seats for the brothers and medieval tiled floor. Melrose Abbey is altogether grander. Founded by David I in 1136, most of what can now be seen is superb decorated architecture of the 15th century. It is a masterpiece of fantastic stone carving from the delicate ogee arches of the cloisters to the carved foliage of the capitals and exquisite vaulting. If anything, the sculpture is even more magnificent, and even mutilation and time have not destroyed the elegant curves of the Virgin and Child. Abbey St Bathans on the other hand turns out never to have had an abbey at all. There was, however, a priory established in the 12th century for 12 nuns and a prioress. The remains were incorporated into the fabric of the parish church, but the effigy of one prioress has survived.

SIR WALTER SCOTT

It is doubtful if very many people read Sir Walter Scott these days: the Waverley novels seem to be permanent features of most second-hand bookshops, glumly gathering dust on the highest, least accessible shelves. Yet he was one of the most popular writers of all time and one of the most influential – and that influence at least is still felt today. The image of the kilted Highlander as one of the most romantic figures in British history comes to us from Scott and, more surprisingly perhaps, so too does the image of the Highlands themselves as representing a beautiful landscape to be enjoyed. Scott was born in 1771 and to most Englishmen – and not a few Scots – the Highlanders were the barbarians who had rebelled against the Crown. The country itself was even less admired. Dr Samuel Johnson, who went on his tour to the Western Isles with Boswell in 1773, was scathing: 'An eye accustomed to flowery pastures and waving harvests is astonished and repelled by this wide extent of hopeless sterility.' Scott gave back dignity to his native history and by the end of his life the heather-covered hills were generally accepted as the finest, most beautiful scenery the British Isles could offer.

Scott, who was born in Edinburgh, suffered ill health, becoming lame in one leg. He was sent off to his grandfather's farm at Sandy Knowe in the Border hills to recover. Here, his grandmother kept him amused with songs and stories of the old days in the Borders. He went on to study law, but the legends stayed with him and in 1800 he wrote 'The Eve of St John', the first of the Border Ballads. His poetry was greeted with immense enthusiasm. 'The Lay of the

Last Minstrel' was so popular that the publishers offered him what was then the immense sum of £1,000 for his next work *Marmion, A Tale of Flodden Field*. In 1814 he published *Waverley*, the first of the Waverley novels. If he did nothing else he put Scotland on the tourist map, as visitors rushed to see the scenes he had described. Walkers along the Southern Upland Way will find no shortage of reminders of Scott and his works.

The first to be met on the Way itself is the Martyrs' Tomb, one of many memorials to the Covenanters who died for their faith and who were commemorated by tablets carved by Robert Paterson, who inspired *Old Mortality*. Close by Butterhole Bridge is a sign to Lochinvar. The loch is now a reservoir, and Lochinvar drowned beneath its waters, but the name is remembered in some of the poet's best-known lines.

O, young Lochinvar is come out of the west,
Through all the wide Border his steed was the best.

On next to Tibbie Shiels Inn, where Scott ate and drank with friends, including fellow poet, James Hogg. Then, it's on to St Mary's Loch, whose description in *Marmion* is still appropriate – on a good day!

For in the mirror, bright and blue,
Each hill's huge outline you might view.

Nearby Dryhope Tower has more robust associations, as home to the notorious border reiver, Auld Wat of Harden, who raided far and wide in the 16th century, and was one of Scott's more disreputable, but much-admired, ancestors. There are many other associations with the author in the region, from romantic St Ronan's Well, which he helped popularize, to the bank in Galashiels, where he kept his money, but nowhere evokes his spirit more clearly than Abbotsford. Scott had a farmhouse on the land, which he pulled down and in its place erected a mansion of turrets and battlements, chock full of armour and weaponry. It recreated in solid form his vision of the heroic past just as he had evoked it in his writings. But mock medievalism had its limits even for Scott: Abbotsford was among the first buildings in Scotland to be lit by gas. Sir Walter Scott was one of the most romantic of all the Romantics, but he was a practical man as well. Abbotsford remained his home until his death in 1832.

Sir Walter Scott's house, Abbotsford, is the equivalent in stone of his own romance

picturesque evocation of former glories.

THE
SOUTHERN
UPLAND
WAY

1 PORTPATRICK TO CASTLE KENNEDY

via Knockquhassen   *13½ miles (21.5 km)*

Portpatrick is a delightful spot, a small harbour created in a naturally sheltered cove, a ring of houses round the bay and a small lighthouse at the entrance. A few fishing boats and pleasure craft and a greater number of oyster catchers still use the harbour, but huge stone bollards are a reminder of the days when this, and not Stranraer, was the port from which vessels left for Ireland. The walk begins up the steps from the end of the little harbour **1** overlooked by a grand, turreted hotel. The route is indicated by the thistle-in-a-hexagon that appears on all direction posts along the Way.

Once up the steps there is a fine prospect of cliffs sending jagged spines of rock out into the sea. At the top of the climb take the path between the old coastguard station and the cliff edge. The path leads through gorse bushes to a road beside the golf course. Turn left along the road, which soon peters out into a broad grassy track, with a view down to a dramatic rock pinnacle. The path gradually narrows and winds its way round the small inlets. It is a most attractive walk taken against a noisy background of shrill piping oyster catchers and squabbling gulls.

The harbour at Portpatrick. The Way begins with a climb up the hill in the background.

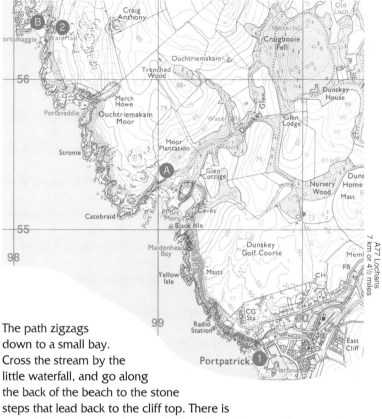

The path zigzags
down to a small bay.
Cross the stream by the
little waterfall, and go along
the back of the beach to the stone
steps that lead back to the cliff top. There is
scarcely time to enjoy the view before the path comes down again to
Port Kale Cove **A**. Here, a curious little building with a double pyra-
midal roof stands at the point where the first telephone cable was laid
under the sea to Ireland in the 1850s.

At the end of the track down to the beach, cross the wooden footbridge and follow the cliffs round towards the sea until a gap in the
rocks appears. Go round the back of a massive rock, and climb the
cliffs by the steep stone steps with a chain hand rail. At the top, the
Way follows a comfortable grassy path, with magnificent views over
to the Irish coast. The path itself is indistinct in places but is clearly
marked by a line of wooden posts. It turns temporarily inland round
the back of a rocky knoll, after which the next main objective,
Killantringan lighthouse **B** comes into view. The Way drops down into
a little gully. Pass through a wooden gate and continue on the cliff-
top path. Just before a steep drop **2**, turn right through a gap in the
stone wall, towards the lighthouse, then turn away from the sea to

follow the edge of the inlet. Down below are the bow and stern, all that remain of the coaster *Craigantlet*, which foundered on the rocks in 1982. Cross a stile and continue up the hill. Cross over the head of the inlet and head for a prominent signpost **3**. At the road turn right. The view along the coast to the north is particularly attractive with sandy beaches backed by low cliffs.

The road now heads inland, through an area of rough pasture for sheep and cattle, and the trilling song of the skylark, which will keep the walker company for much of the way, is heard for the first time. At the T-junction **4** turn left onto the main road and then after a short way turn right onto the minor road **5**, with a standing stone in the field at the corner. As the road climbs, views open out with rolling farmland and moor to the right and the sea to the left. The road passes Knock and Maize Cottage – a romantic name, mundanely meaning 'hillock and bog' – and then swings sharply to the left **6**. At this point double right back onto the track at the right. At the top of the hill where the Way divides by ruined buildings, continue straight on, along a grassy track. Crossing a stile, the Way follows the line of a ditch and bank topped with gorse, from

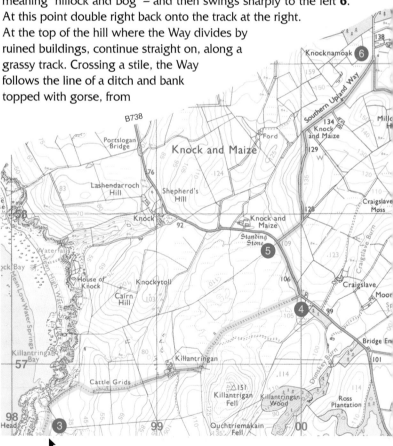

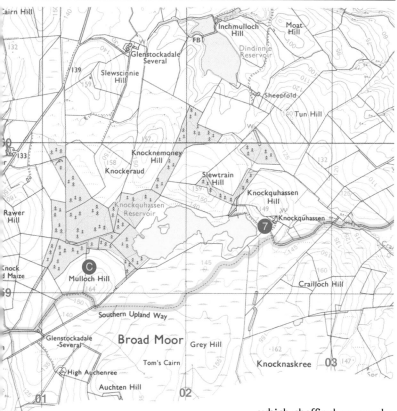

which chaffinch serenade the passer-by. Head straight to the top of the hill **C**, from where there is a view right across to the peaks of Arran and the curious little rock shaped like a fancy cake, Ailsa Craig. Turn off to the right and, descending the hill, a stile comes into view with the next stage of the Way appearing as an obvious path through the moorland, with a sight of high hills in the distance. The path goes through tussocky grass, heather and dark, peaty pools, and the songs of curlew, lapwing and lark vie for attention. After a great deal of jiggling around, the path eventually reaches the eastern end of Knockquhassen Reservoir. Follow the fence at the waterside, and head for the gap between a clump of conifers and a rocky outcrop. As the moorland ends **7**, turn right onto the farm track.

The sea now appears again up ahead as the Way crosses the narrow neck of land known as The Rhins. The nature of the route also changes as it takes on more of the character of a country lane. With thorn hedges to either side, it could seem more English than Scottish,

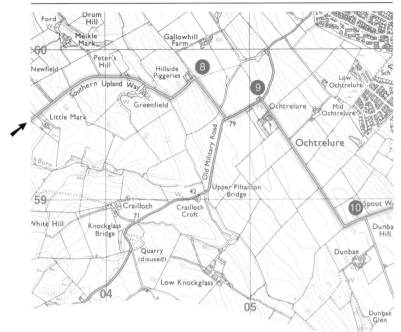

but for the shaggy black cattle in the
fields. At Little Mark Farm the track becomes a
surfaced farm road, which continues straight on up to a T-junction **8**.
Turn right, then almost immediately left at the next junction. At the
top of the little hill, Stranraer with its Irish ferry traffic comes into view
at the head of Loch Ryan. Turn right up the quiet lane **9**, with hedges
to either side. Now the view opens right out down the loch with Ailsa
Craig standing guard at the entrance. The road turns sharp left, and
then, as it turns sharp right **10**, continue straight on along the footpath leading gently downhill with the gorse hedge to the side. At the
road, turn right **11**. The road swings round to go through the gap in
the embankment of the old Portpatrick and Wigtownshire Railway **D**;
the Portpatrick to Stranraer section was closed in 1950. At the main
road **12** turn left and almost immediately right onto the track that runs
alongside the copse. At the end of the track **13** there is a dog-leg,
turning right onto the road, then left onto another farm track. A
marshy pool to the left is home to wildfowl, including Canada geese.
At the junction **14** turn left onto the track beside the wood, where
grand beech contrast with delicate silver birch. The track then swings
right to go through the wood and then turns right where the track
divides **15**. By the next patch of wood, a small loch can be glimpsed
as a gleam of water through the trees.

The peaceful lock at Knockquhassen marks the halfway point on the walk across the Rhins.

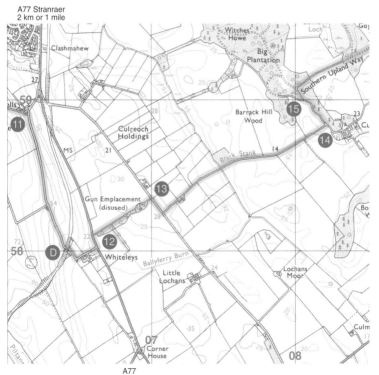

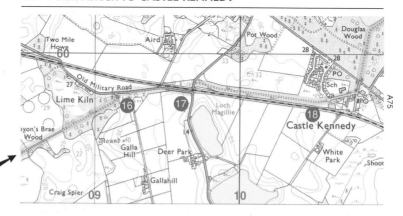

Leave the wood by the lodge **16** and turn right onto the road. At the T-junction **17** turn left under the railway and halfway up the little hill turn right onto the footpath beside the tracks. This is the still active part of the line already encountered, and which ends at Stranraer. Leave the woods by the houses at the edge of Castle Kennedy **18** and continue straight on along the road to the main road.

An avenue of trees creates the formal approach to the White Loch and Castle Kennedy.

2 Castle Kennedy to Bargrennan

via Polbae and Knowe

26½ miles (43 km)

This is a long section, but it is possible to break it into two sections by turning off to New Luce. Cross over the main road **19** and continue straight on along the driveway through the Castle Kennedy grounds, a formal approach down an avenue of trees, interspersed with brilliant clumps of rhododendra. The old, gaunt 17th-century castle **A** contrasts oddly with the luxuriant parkland that now surrounds it. As the drive reaches the loch, it swings round to the right and there is a view of the grandiloquent Scottish baronial pile of Lochinch Castle. The Way goes through the attractive landscaped grounds and then turns off to the right by the main entrance and the coach park. Over to the left is Loch Crindil, with a little island that is actually a crannog, an artificial platform built up out of the shallow waters for homes during the Iron Age.

At the road **20** turn left. Cults Loch, to the side of the road, also has a crannog, home to a variety of wildfowl rather than Iron Age families. Just before the road turns to the right **21** take the broad track to the right that leads past the cottages, passing through an area of rich pasture for

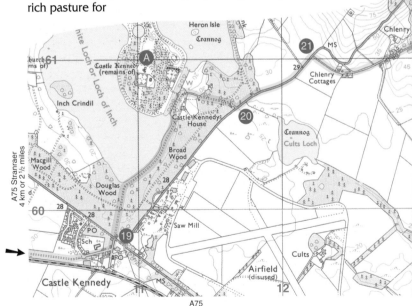

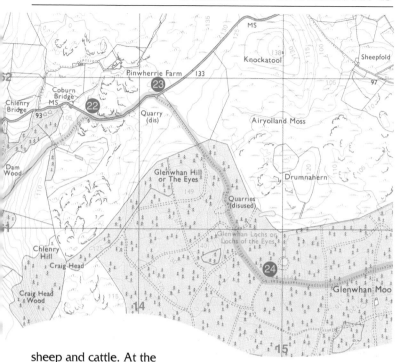

sheep and cattle. At the
entrance to the imposing house of
Chlenry, go straight on to cross the bridge over the stream and continue through the farm buildings. The track now climbs up through a
small conifer plantation. At the far side, cross the stile and continue
straight on following the line of the wall. This is a steady climb with
wide views, and the walker is likely to see pheasants abandoning the
woods for a stroll through the fields. At the top of the hill, a vista of
smooth, green hills, patched with conifers opens out. Continue to a
ladder stile, cross it and continue in the same direction. After crossing a second stile, the track runs straight ahead over an area of rough
grass and peaty moorland, studded with boulders. At the road **22**
turn right. This is a rugged landscape with rocky outcrops that provide wind breaks for stunted gorse bushes. At a small parking space
at the top of the hill **23** turn right onto the broad track leading off
towards the forest. It is worth lingering over this section to enjoy the
wide views before the trees take over.

The path plunges into dense, dark forest where birdsong fills the air,
but the singers remain invisible among the close-packed trees. An old
quarry provides a break, and then after a somewhat claustrophobic
start, the view opens up a little. Where the track divides **24** turn left,

and then, where the main track swings round in a big curve **25**, turn off to the right onto a narrower, rougher path of humps and hollows, peaty bogs and little streams. The path arrives at the edge of the wood **B** with a rather surprising view of the sea at Luce Sands. Turn left to follow the line of the wall along a narrow and very squelching path, which soon swings away from the wall and begins to go downhill. Ahead, there are glimpses of hills and a more open landscape. By a wooden marker post **26** turn left to head even more steeply down through the trees on a path that soon begins to zigzag to reduce the angle of the slope.

At the foot of the hill, follow the path round to the left through a pleasant area of mixed woodland. The Way now runs along a ledge on the hillside, with the railway visible down below. Where the way is barred by a small fence, turn right to follow the less distinct path through the trees. It swings round to the left and a cheerful burbling announces the arrival of a stream

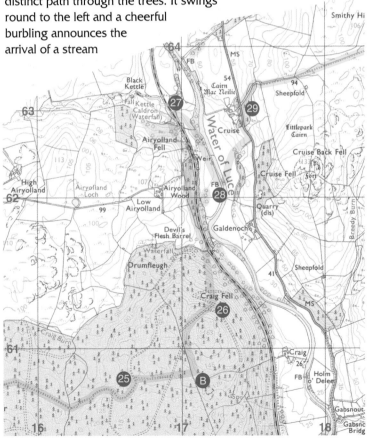

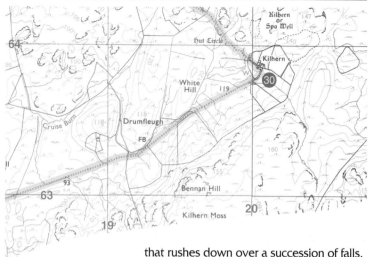

that rushes down over a succession of falls.
Cross the bridge and a stile and continue straight up the hill
opposite, into an area of old oak woodland. At the edge of the
wood cross the stile and turn left through the gap in the wall, still following the line of the railway. Now the wood begins to thin out, leaving space for woodland flowers, wood anemone and bluebells to
flourish. Leaving the wood by a stile, turn right to follow the fence
round to a second stile and then turn right to cross the railway **27**
over a little cutting blasted out of the rock.

Take the path down the grassy slope to the river bank, where the
honey-coloured peaty water bounces along over its stony bed. Turn
right at the bank to follow the river down to the attractive wooden suspension bridge **28**. Cross over and head diagonally up the field to the
prominent white hexagon marker at the edge of the wood. Cross the
stile, follow the path up beside the gully to the corner of the field and
turn left onto the road. At this point it is possible to keep on the road
up to New Luce. The Way, however, only goes a short way up the road
before turning right immediately beyond the farm **29** onto the broad
track running up beside the wood. At the top of the slope, cross the
stile and continue alongside the stone wall. Now the view opens out to
a great swell of hills, with farmland reaching almost to the tops where
the rough moor takes over. Soon the fields are left behind as the track
runs straight and true towards the ruins of a small farm, set amid a web
of walls. At first this is very squelchy going, but beyond a ladder stile
the path improves, and there are little dark burns to either side. At the
farm **30** turn left to pass in front of the buildings; do not follow the more
obvious track through the farmyard. This is now very pleasant walking

on grassland between pale rock outcrops. Go through an iron gate and stay with the track as it sweeps round a small plantation on its way down to the road **31**. Again there is an opportunity to visit New Luce by turning left, but the Way itself goes to the right along the road.

The road now runs alongside the river with attractive falls **C** that can best be seen from the footbridge. Where the road divides **32** continue straight on along the road shown as a dead end. The river, which has swung away, now returns, and the Way begins to climb up from the smooth green fields, by a straggle of stunted trees, to the tussocky upland. Here, land divisions are very clear: the rich valley parcelled out into neat fields that extend to the edge of the moor and a much more open landscape, dotted with the occasional, lonely farm. Balmurrie is typical, a whitewashed house with dormer windows and a protective shelter of trees. At the farm continue straight on along the track to the left of the barn. After a short way, the main track swings round to the left and then immediately beyond the stone wall **33** turns right onto a rather vague path beside the wall. This is pleasant, upland walking through pale, spiky grass interspersed with peaty streams and pools. The wall acts as a kind of boundary: grass on one side, heather on the other, and there are promises of even more dramatic scenery in the hills up ahead. At the top of a rise, the path heads away from the wall towards a ladder stile. Once that is crossed, head to the left of the hillock ahead. The Way cuts a green swathe through the pallid moorland grasses to head for another rise, which offers an all-round view that includes the dark mass of forest that crosses the Way. The path heads for the woodland and swings right for the wide gap in the trees.

Approaching Water of Luce from Craig Fell.

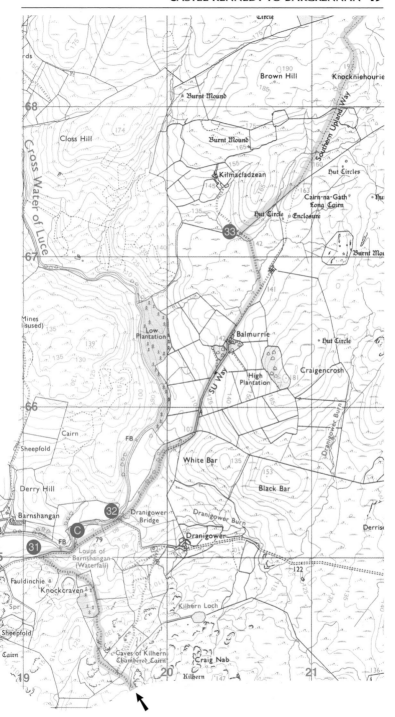

The ancient standing stones of Laggangarn with later Christian crosses.

Cross the stile **34** and head into conifer forest that is to be the dominant feature for the rest of this section. The Way follows a broad track that crosses a small stream, and is sufficiently open to allow enticing views of the surrounding hills. At the open space, take the obvious track to the left, which comes down to a stony forest road **35** and turn right. There are still wide views to enjoy, but where the track begins to turn left and head uphill **36** turn right onto a narrower, grassy track, altogether rougher going, with boggy peat and tussocks. At the stone wall, turn left and cross the wall at a broken-down section to continue in the same direction on the opposite side. Cross again at the corner of two walls and the path leads into a clearing **D** where a curious, wigwam-like wooden shelter, known as 'The Beehive', offers overnight shelter for walkers. Continue on through the clear gap in the trees and an even more obvious landmark appears up ahead in the form of two tall standing stones **E**. These are the standing stones of Laggangarn and were probably erected in the New Stone Age some 4,000 years ago, and were adopted in the Dark Ages by pilgrims who carved crosses on them.

Cross the footbridge over Tarf Water and the taller trees now close in on the path, a raised stony way that keeps your feet clear of the surrounding peat bog. There are occasional views of the fell to the right. At the top of the hill, a signpost points off to the Wells of the Rees where it is said lepers from Glenluce Abbey came for the curative waters. The top of the hill is marked by a cairn like a Jacobean chimney pot, a good place to pause and enjoy the panoramic views **F**. Here the path turns to the left along the obvious stony track. At the

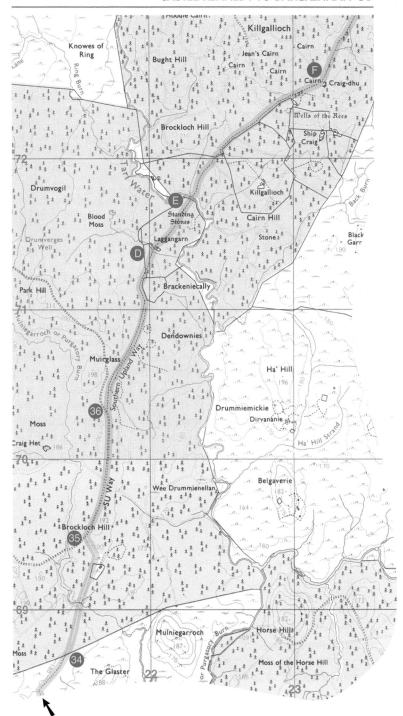

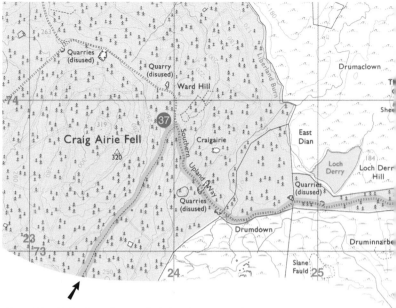

Craig Airie Fell is heavily wooded, but there are still superb views out across the surrounding fells.

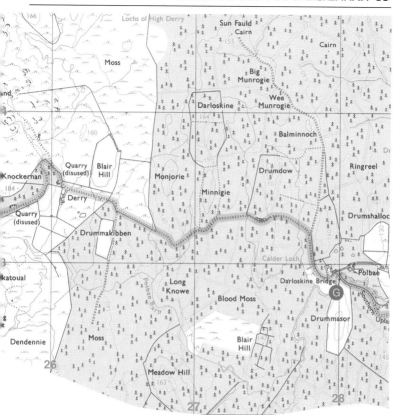

broad forest road **37** turn right. It eventually runs down to the forest edge, and a marker points the way out to Linn's Grave, the tomb of a Covenant Martyr, about half a mile from the Way. Soon the trees clear altogether giving an overwhelming impression of an empty landscape, when quite suddenly, it seems, the moorland ends in a chequerboard of fields surrounding a trim farmhouse. The path turns away, however, towards a rocky hill topped with a cairn and then swings all the way round to arrive back at the farm again.

Now the nature of the section changes once more as the rough track gives way to a metalled road. The trees are well set back, and the river meanders lazily, cutting a serpentine path through the woods. Where the river is crossed **G** there is a ruined lodge and the somewhat dilapidated house of Polbae, among what must once have been spectacular grounds with mature trees, rhododendra and an ornamental lake. After that it is a return to the more familiar conifers.

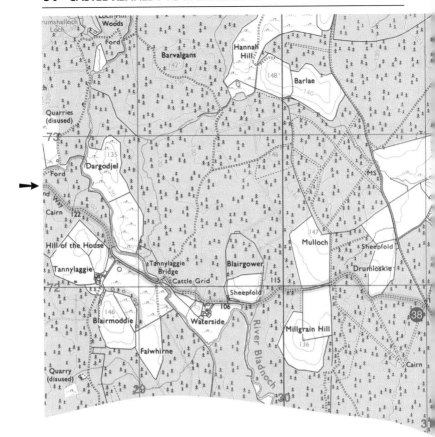

Then, just as one is beginning to be bored with the forest scene, the view opens out again to a fine stand of pine, and the River Bladnoch reappears with a steep, grassy hill rising above it, where herons stand sentry duty on the bank. The river is recrossed on a sturdy stone bridge, and now the Bladnoch goes off in a series of extravagant bends. Farmland pops up among the trees and the high hills are now a good deal nearer. At the road junction **38** turn right.

The route passes through the hamlet of Knowe, where an old milestone informs the traveller that Newton Stewart is 8 miles away. Cross the bridge over the burn **39** and turn left onto the little grass footpath that winds through the trees. It crosses a major forest road and arrives at a clearing where it heads right round a hillock. At the next clearing, the path takes an obvious swing to the right and then turns almost immediately left for the stile and the wire fence to take the stony path to the clump of beech trees. At the road **40** turn left.

At first there is still forest to the left, but when that ends there are sweeping views over the moors and on to the distant hills. Glenruther Farm appears sitting comfortably among sheltering trees, then the road heads off to a stretch of empty moor, with little to disturb the quest but the plaintive cries of curlew. Then, just past the cattle grid **41**, turn right onto a path over the moor, with a fine view down over Loch Ochiltree. It goes up the rise, making for the cairn at the top of the hill, which offers a complete panorama of the surrounding country.

The path now continues across the moor, waymarked by a line of posts. Once over a rise, a long stone wall comes into view on the right and the path heads diagonally towards it, crosses a small footbridge and then follows the line of the wall. Cross a ladder stile and continue following the wall for a short way, before turning left by a marker post to head for the left-hand side of the wood. The path follows the edge of the wood for a short way then dives in among the trees. This is a grotesque Brothers Grimm sort of wood, with gnarled trees, mossy stumps and dark boulders.

A wooden footbridge crossing the busy Water of Trool near the junction with Water of Minnoch.

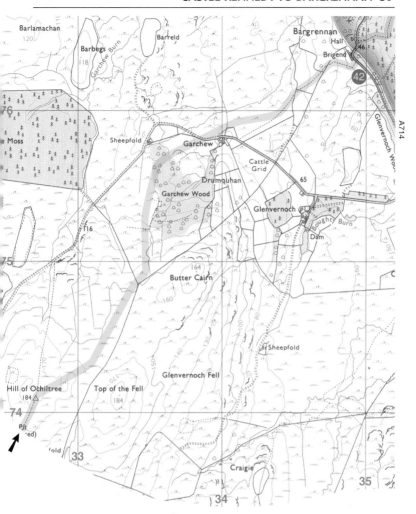

On leaving the wood, head for the ladder stile in the wall opposite and cross over the road. The track runs at an angle from the road, initially heading to the right of the house snuggled down among the trees. The path follows a little burn for a while, to head towards a ladder stile. Once over the next stile it tops a small hillock, and more stiles appear, ending with one to the right of the house **42**, which leads down onto the road. Turn left to cross the bridge over the river. Those in search of refreshment should continue on this road to the inn, but the Way turns right onto the forest track.

3 BARGRENNAN TO ST JOHN'S TOWN OF DALRY

via Loch Trool   *22½ miles (31 km)*

The section begins on a broad forest track, but then almost immediately turns left onto a stony path that swings round to the right. It goes uphill between tall pines, and turns left at the top of the hill and then at once begins swinging away to the right on a rather rough, heavily churned-up track. At the stone wall **43** turn right, cross through the wall and continue following the line of the wall up the hill. This is much easier going on a grassy track, with dense plantations to either side. At the top, the trees thin out and there is a chance to admire the view across the hills. The track swings off to the left and continues on to the road **44**. Cross straight over and continue on the narrow path beside the stone wall. Now the conifers give way to a hummocky woodland dominated by oak and birch, which is very popular with the local chaffinches.

The path leads down to the Water of Minnoch. Cross over the bridge **45** and turn left to follow the line of the river. This is a very pleasant stroll through broad-leaved woodland, with the burble of the river never very far away. Then the path comes right down to the bank of the broad river splashing over shallows. Across the water cattle graze the fields and dippers bob their heads politely from the rocks.

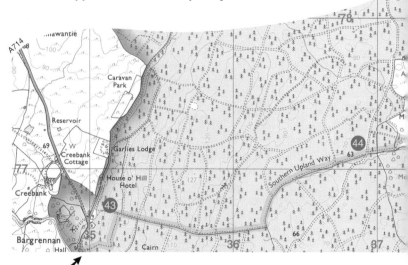

Now the path climbs a small hillock **A** where a seat has been thought-fully provided for those who want to pause and enjoy this most attractive spot where the Water of Trool joins the Minnoch. The route continues alongside the river, which after a busy dash down small falls, saunters languorously along past reed beds that the path skirts. It returns to the waterside as a comfortable, grassy track and then heads into a young birch woodland where the river is reduced to a stream as it passes round a large island **46**. Now the path becomes more wayward, as it winds through a wood cut by small streams and then climbs a small knoll, which provides a wide view of a forest-dominated landscape, the trees climbing almost to the summit of the surrounding hills. It wobbles off again through the trees, and eventually reaches a stile at the edge of the camp site. From here a short diversion down a paved path to the right leads to the Martyr's Tomb, a curious affair where the memorial to six Covenanters caught at prayer and massacred by soldiers is hidden behind high stone walls **B**.

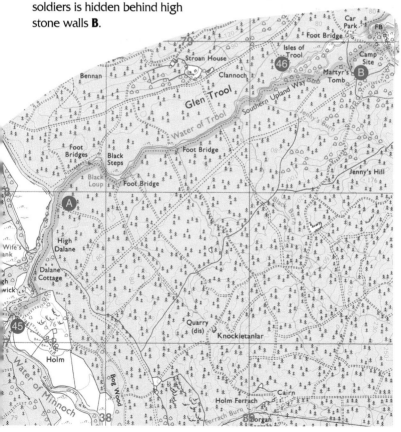

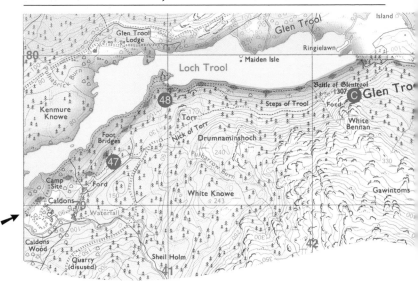

The path now heads through the camp site, past the toilet blocks, to arrive at the other side as a stony path that turns away from the loch to climb a small knoll with a view down over the water **47**. The track turns back downhill at a gentle angle to rejoin the loch shore. It remains on the loch side on a narrow way with a steep, heavily wooded slope rising above it. This would be a delightfully peaceful walk if it were not for the rowdy, quarrelsome gulls who have taken up residence on the loch. The going can be quite difficult: veterans of the West Highland Way will be strongly reminded of the Loch Lomond path as they scrabble around and hop over boulders. A short way beyond the peninsula that sticks out into the loch **48**, the Way follows a new route opened in 1996. Instead of following a forest track at a higher level, it stays at the loch side all the way. Near the end of the loch it is worth glancing up the hillside to think of what it must have been like for the English soldiers trudging through the hills suddenly to be confronted by Highlanders racing down on them from the heights. For this **C** is the site of the Battle of Trool. At the end of the loch, the path continues straight on to join the Glenhead Burn **49**, where it reunites with the older, high-level walk. This is an attractive and interesting section: the burn gurgles cheerfully, and it is worth looking out for wild goats and red squirrels in the woods. Across the water is rough moorland, while up ahead the hills pile up. Where two streams meet **50**, turn right to follow the path into the forest. It climbs up steeply beside a boldly leaping mountain stream to a forest road **51**. Turn left onto this road, which will now be followed for many miles.

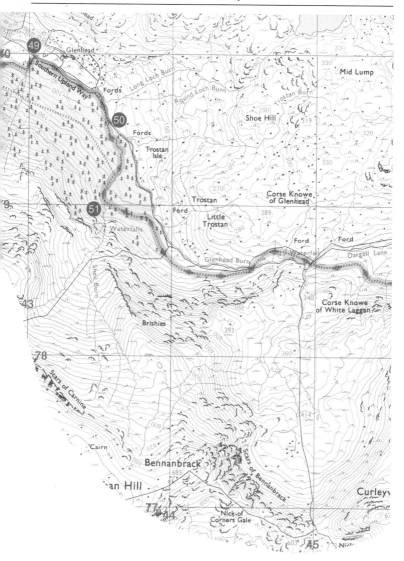

The nature of the landscape changes quite dramatically. The hills have craggy faces, down one of which a waterfall slices as a thin, white streak. When the forest ends, the track has the character of a true mountain pass, and it is worthwhile pausing to look back on Loch Trool and its surrounding hills. At the top of the pass, another mountain stream plunges down the hill in a series of falls, and a new view opens

Loch Trool. There are plenty of opportunities to enjoy this fine scenery as the path stays close to the water's edge.

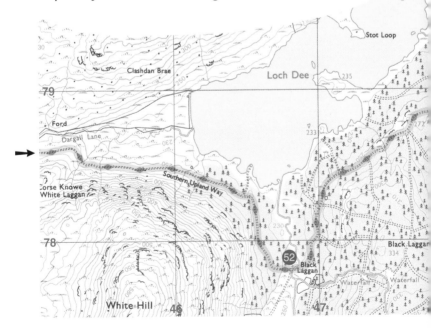

up over Loch Dee. After this fine open section, the trees reappear, but sufficiently sparse still to allow views of the loch for a while. Then they close in completely as the path swings away into the forest. There is a break by the anglers' lodge and a seat to enjoy the view.

A track from the Black Laggan Burn **52** leads south to the White Laggan bothy. This section of the Way is undeniably something of a trudge, but at least the trees are well set back and there are views out over the hills. Where the way divides by a circular sheep fold **53** turn left to cross the river, and follow the track round to the right. This is a brief respite before the conifers close in again, and there is no real

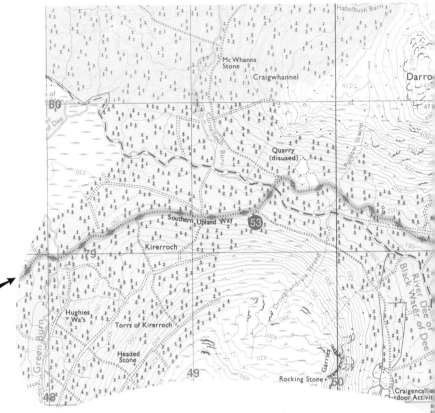

Bruce's Stone: the Way runs along the opposite shore.

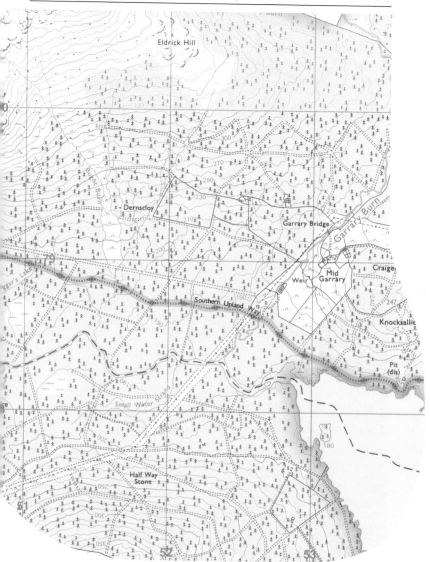

break until the swathe cut for power lines and pylons, which also provides the first glimpse of a house for many a mile. Eventually, relief from the monotony arrives with the first glimpse of Clatteringshaws Loch. It is a peaceful spot, with a broad expanse of water, but surprisingly, no obvious sign of waterfowl. The lochside visit is brief, and soon the track swings away to the left and more conifers before it

The gentle farmland near St John's Town of Dalry with a background of imposing hi

The wild beauty of Clatteringshaws Loch is especially welcome as it comes at the end of a long forest trail.

finally arrives at a road **54**. This marks the end of one of the longest, uninterrupted sections along the Way.

Turn left onto the road and enjoy the open spaces for a while, then turn off to cross the stile by the stone wall on the right **55**. Following the line of the wall and continuing on a stony track, the road heads, seemingly inevitably, back towards the next patch of forest. Once in the woodland, although the trees are set well back, the only view is of still vaster expanses of forest. Then, after climbing a little hill, the whole character changes. There are views of the surrounding hills, and the path heads down through the trees to an exciting prospect of wild moorland ahead. It is a robust landscape, with a jagged edge to the horizon where rocks and boulders stick through and the splendidly named Meikle Lump and neighbouring Meikle Millyea dominate the scene. A peaty path passes through tussocks up the rocky hillside, and at the top of the rise the view opens to the next range of hills: but before that comes the next swathe of spruce.

A broad farm track leads down the hill and crosses a burn. At the farm track near the house **56** turn right, cross a stream and follow the track round the edge of the wood. The path follows the line of a little

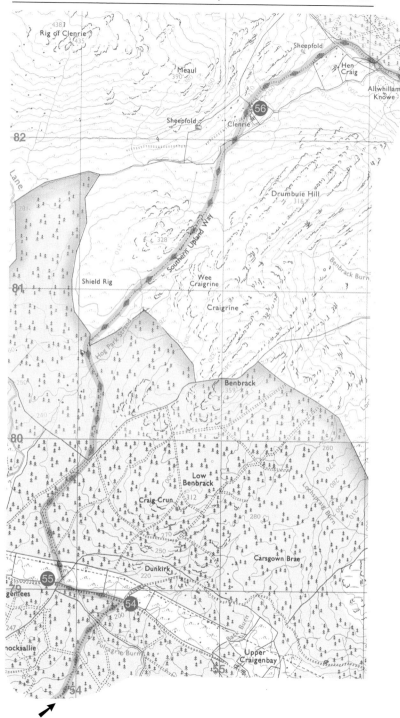

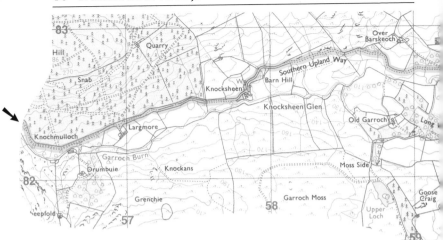

burn, with a grassy hill rising steeply above it. The track becomes a metalled road that continues the route beside the wood. Soon the forest ends at the left and the burn wanders away to the right, revealing a gentler country of grassy slopes measured out into fields by dry-stone walls. With the richer pasture, farms appear at ever shorter intervals. The road now twists and turns through woodland, largely of oak, birch and hawthorn with spatterings of woodland flowers. The burn reappears to run alongside the road, dashing and darting through the rocks under a canopy of trees. Eventually, the road crosses the stream on a little stone bridge crowded round with rhododendra. At the top of the next hill **57** turn left to take the path by the stone wall, back down to the burn.

The path follows the stream, crosses it by a footbridge and then continues in the same direction on the opposite bank. A stile leads into the field and duck boards ease the way over boggy ground. From a stile in the corner of the field, take the path up over the hill. Breasting the rise, head down towards the pylon by the sheepfold and the next target, the power station, appears down below **58**. The path runs beside the water cascading down from the dam at Earlstoun Loch. At the road turn right; St John's Town of Dalry can be seen across the fields. At the far end of the very large field **59** turn left where the fence meets the road and follow the path down to the suspension bridge. Looking back, the pipelines that carry the water down to the power station can be seen. Crossing the bridge, the path passes between a Norman motte or mound, which would have been topped with defensive works of wood or stone and the rather ornate 19th-century church bristling with pinnacles. It leads straight up to the centre of St John's Town of Dalry.

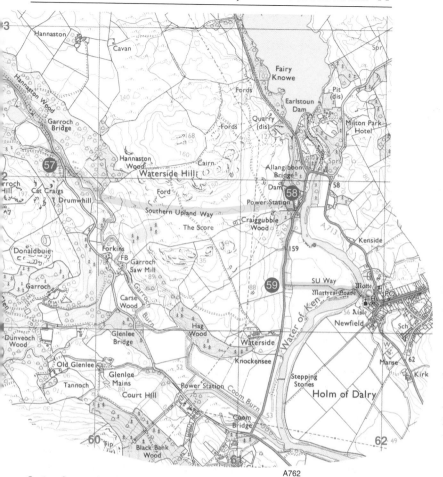

A762

Spring flowers brighten the wayside near St John's Town of Dalry.

The suspension bridge across the Water of Ken at St John's Town of Dalry.

4 ST JOHN'S TOWN OF DALRY TO SANQUHAR

via Butterhole Bridge and Allan's Cairn   *25 miles (40 km)*

The next section is one of the most demanding of the whole Southern Upland Way, and those who are unsure about their fitness and stamina should try and make arrangements to break it down into two sections. It begins innocently enough with a stroll up the broad main street, lined with typical Scottish vernacular houses. At the end of the town, where the road swings round to the right **60**, turn left along the road marked as a dead end and then continue straight on as it deteriorates into a rougher road that in turn becomes a track between stone walls. As the houses end, so the path begins to climb past patches of gorse and a wood boasting one massive old beech tree. At the top of the hill a wide expanse of moorland spreads out ahead and rounded hills swell up to the right. The route continues following the line of the wall, but the view is constantly changing, sometimes closed in by little rocky hummocks, but more often offering grander views of the spreading hills.

After crossing a ladder stile continue following the wall and at the next cross wall **61** look for a ladder stile on the left and turn diagonally across the field in the direction of the house in front of the trees. At the next ladder stile, head straight up the hill opposite, the climb eased by the comfortable footing of springy turf. Once over the hill, continue down to the stile by the farm gate and join the track by the wall. The track runs right past the house with its array of dormer windows to take the path to the left, running up between stone walls. Where the track divides **62** take the turning to the right, which runs along the rim of a little wooded valley with a stream at the bottom – another place where red squirrels were spotted. Once over the next stile, the Way leaves the farm track to continue along the valley edge for a while, then, immediately after going through a gap in the stone wall, turns slightly left away from the gully towards a Way post with a conifer plantation beyond. Once over the rise the next ladder stile appears in view. This is still splendid, rolling grassland, offering rough grazing for sheep, and is dotted with isolated farms. The actual path is not particularly clear, but runs roughly parallel to the forest boundary wall. Eventually, the path leads down to a ladder stile with a footbridge beyond it. Once over the bridge turn right to cross a second stile and continue beside the fence. The route follows a little burn that winds gently down a shallow valley.

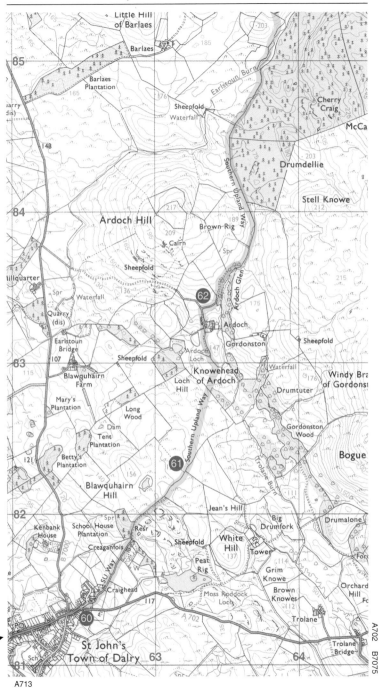

Little Hill
of Barlaes

Barlaes

Barlaes
Plantation

203

185

85

Quarry
(dis)

148

165

176

Earlstoun Burn

Sheepfold

Waterfall

Cherry
Craig

McCa

Drumdellie

203

Stell Knowe
212

84

Ardoch Hill

217

Brown-Rig

189

Southern Upland Way

209

Cairn

Spr

215

Sheepfold

Waterfall

136

llquarter

Spr

Quarry
(dis)

Earlstoun
Bridge

107

Sheepfold

Ardoch Glen

175

62

Ardoch

Gordonston

Sheepfold

Ardoch
Loch

147

83

115

Blawquhairn
Farm

Mary's
Plantation

Long
Wood

Dam

Tent
Plantation

121

Betty's
Plantation

156

Blawquhairn
Hill

Knowehead
of Ardoch

Loch
Hill

Waterfall

176

Windy Bra
of Gordons

Drumtuter

Gordonston
Wood

Bogue

Southern Upland Way

61

Jean's Hill

Trolane Burn

82

Kenbank
House

School House
Plantation

Resr

Creaganfois

Spr

SU Way

B7000

Craighead

Big
Drumfork

White
Hill
137

Tower

Sheepfold

Peat
Rig

114

Grim
Knowe

Brown
Knowes

Trolane

Drumalone

For

Orchard
Hill

Fo

117

126

Moss Roddock
Loch

112

60

PO

St John's
Town of Dalry

Sch

63

A702

A713

64

Trolane
Bridge

A702

B7075

81

The Way then goes steeply uphill and from the top of the rise, the path can be seen heading for the saddle of the double-humped hill ahead. After crossing a stream, the path is clearer for a while, and then swings round to the left to meet a rise and heads down at an angle to the road. Route finding in good visibility is not as difficult as these rather complex directions might make it appear.

Coming off the moor **63**, continue in the same direction up the road opposite. This is a lonely moorland road that climbs slowly and steadily. Cross over attractively named Butterhole Bridge, beyond which there is a turning down to the Blackwater Bridge Youth Hostel. The Way, however, continues forward to the top of the hill. Then, where a plantation appears on the right **64** turn left to take the path that heads straight up the hillside. After a short steep climb, another wide spread of moor appears with a distant post on the horizon as a waymark. The Way is

The lonely moorland road near Butterhole Bridge. The Way turns off to the left towards the hills.

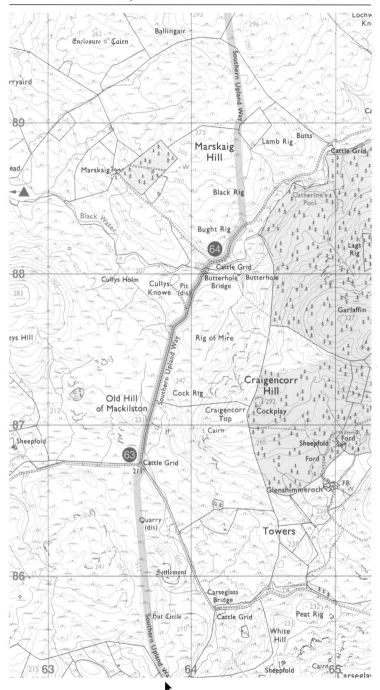

well marked, and the next obvious point to aim for is the corner where a wall joins a fence. Cross over the stile and follow the path round to the right until halfway along it, then turn left towards a just-visible ladder stile. Head slightly to the left of the hummock, where a farmhouse in the middle distance provides a useful reference point to aim for. Once again this is all very open walking with splendid views of the surrounding hills. Eventually, a nearer farmhouse **65** comes into view, and the Way goes past it and through the farmyard to cross a ladder stile and join the farm track that leads down to the road **66.**

At the road, turn right and then left at the next farm. Go up the farm track, and turn left immediately before the gate in the wall to cross the stile and follow the path up beside the wall and round to the right. There is now a long but steady climb, the path running roughly parallel to the wall. On the whole this is easy walking on springy turf, with occasional intrusions of peaty bog where small streams drain off

Two familiar features of the Southern Upland Way: the ladder stile and the thistle-in-a-hexagon waymarker.

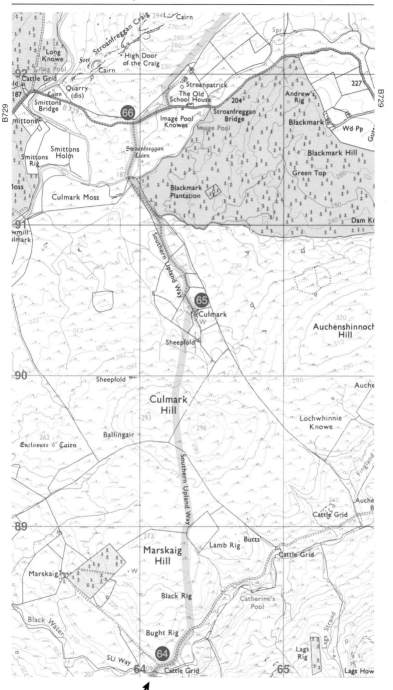

Youth hostels provide attractive accommodation at different points along the Way. This is the Broadmeadows Hostel.

the hill. The next immediate objective is the sheepfold to the right of a small patch of conifers, and a stile comes into view. After crossing the stile, continue along the wall. Drainage ditches have been cut, revealing the dense black peat that forms the top surface of these hills, and the moorland character asserts itself as the turf gives way to tussocks and heather. The path now heads off to pass to the right of the rocky summit of the hill up ahead. Where a new conifer plantation has been started **67**, the path swings left towards the top of Manquhill Hill. This is all still one long climb, and after a steep section it crosses a forest road, goes past a rocky knoll and the path now cuts a green swathe through the pallid grass dotted with young trees.

From the summit plateau **A** you get one of the best viewpoints of the walk so far, with an exhilarating sight of the range of hills to the north and the perhaps less appealing view of the next band of conifers stretching across the way ahead. Closer to hand, peaty pools dot the route; they are so dark and impenetrable that there is no way of telling if they are six inches or six feet deep. The path crosses the shoulder of the hill topped by a cluster of rocks. Topping the rise, there is the slightly daunting prospect of an even higher hill up ahead. The path passes through an area of new plantations, and more peaty ponds, which attract busy water boatmen, who scull across the surface. The Way continues uphill, crossing two forest roads, and although the path

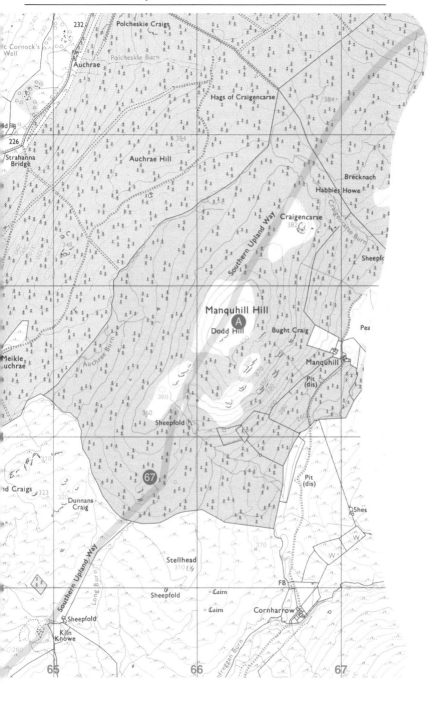

is indistinct it always heads for the obvious summit. Nearing the top, a reassuring marker post appears and the path runs parallel to the forest fence on the left. This long uphill section, which has risen over a thousand feet to a cairn on Benbrack summit **B** at 1,903 feet (580 metres), rewards effort by an even grander view than that from Manquhill Hill.

Cross over the stile and turn left to set off downhill, following the line of the fence. This is still glorious wild open country, with lark song to pipe the walker along. The path turns right, still following the fence, along a bumpy ridge. Soon the view opens out on the right towards a lovely valley scooped out of the hills. There is another chance to pause and admire the scenery at the top of Cairn Hill **C**. Now the Way begins to descend in earnest. The path turns to the right to follow the line of the fence downhill, and, at the edge of the plantation **68**, it turns left onto the broad grassy track that follows the edge of the woodland. Do not follow the obvious stony track that goes into the forest, but continue on the same line beside the fence. The Way then turns right following the clear straight broad track through the forest. This continues straight on, all the way to Allan's Cairn **D**. This is a red sandstone pillar, covered in texts, commemorating George Allan and Margaret Gracie, Covenanters shot by dragoons.

At this point, the Way turns round to the left as a gravelly path through the trees, with banks of heather on either side. It swings to

The lonely moorland road by the Polskeoch Burn.

either side, first left, then right as an altogether humpier route down a fire break and then takes a more pronounced left turn **69** to a clearing where it turns again to head downhill. At the forest road **70** turn right to continue a steady descent. There is a view now to the left, where a burn runs through the heather, and an old sheepfold is a reminder of the days when this was all rough grazing, not forest. The track takes a gentle line through a hairpin bend, passing the Chalk Memorial bothy, which offers rough but often very welcome shelter. Once down at the valley floor, the Way crosses a footbridge and turns right. Where the Way divides **71**, take the path to the right to cross the stream by the sheepfold.

The nature of the walk now changes. Instead of a high-level, rough walk over the moors, there is now a stroll down the centre of a valley, with gently sloping hills to either side. Soon, the first house to be met for some time appears, and at Polskeoch the rough track gives way to a metalled road. Woodland is still a constant companion, but the wider space gives a chance to see the bird life, and with luck a short-eared owl may be seen heading out from the trees with a seemingly lazy flap of its wings, as it sets out on a hunting mission.

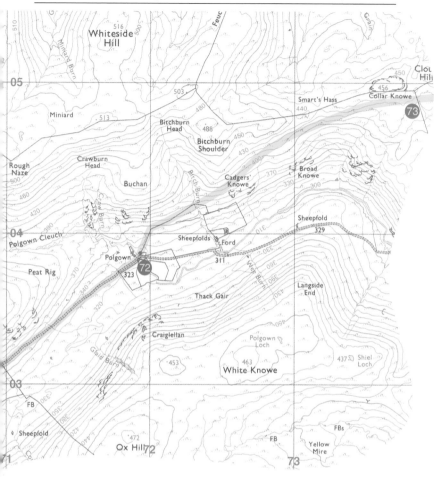

The uniformity of the conifers has been broken by some new plantings of broad-leaved trees. The road soon begins to climb again into open country and the voice of the curlew adds a descant to the chorus of bleating sheep. Soon, the smooth hillside is broken by jagged rocks as the road advances up the shoulder of the hill. At Polgown farm **72**, cross over the burn, turn left beside the sheepfold and then right to follow the line of the fence uphill. After a little way, cross a stile and continue in the same direction, but on the opposite side of the fence. The path climbs gently but steadily round the shoulder of the hill, keeping the peak to the left. It passes to the left of a little dip in the slope, from where there is a delightful view of a narrow valley thrust down between steep hillsides. Now the path heads slightly left, cutting across the hill at a steeper angle towards a stile **73**. The next objective to aim for is a

The track leading down to the farms of Stroanpatrick. The Way heads up over the hill

the right.

spot a little to the right of the pointed peak in the distance. The path now begins to turn left to head downhill, leaving the crags to the left. At the bottom of this hill, cross another ladder stile and take the path that runs away at an angle to the wall through a splendidly lumpy and rocky landscape of grey sandstone with a view over gentler hills and a valley of green fields. Crossing over a hillock, first seen as a blip on the horizon, head off towards a stile by a gate. At the stile turn left over a little mound, from which the end of this section, the town of Sanquhar, comes into view. After all the climbs of the day, it is undeniably pleasant to be faced by a broad, grassy track heading straight downhill.

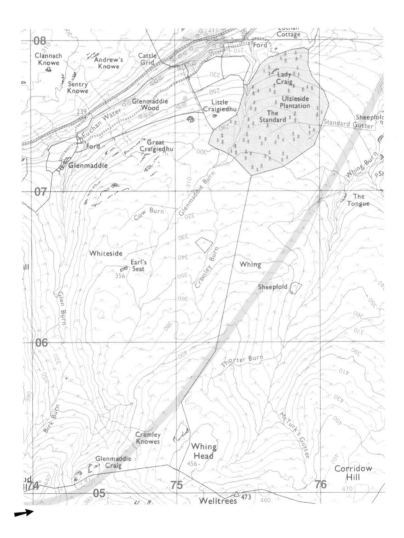

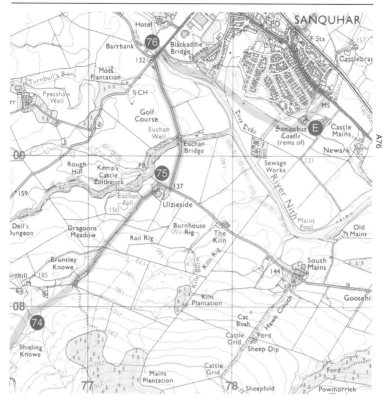

At the foot of the hill head for the farm gate and the stile next to it. Turn right along the path by the fence and then turn diagonally across the field to the gate, heading towards the house. As you get nearer, you will see a stile to the right of the gate in the fence. Cross that and make your way down to the footbridge over the bustling little Whing Burn **74**. The path climbs back out of the gully and leads past sheep pens towards a ladder stile, and after two more stiles the Way joins a track that leads down to the farm by the road **75**.

At the road turn left towards Sanquhar, crossing Euchan Water with its border of oak and pine and continue on over the triple-arched bridge over the Nith **76**. Once over the bridge turn right onto the path beside the big notice board and shelter, and continue on the riverside walk behind the houses to Sanquhar Castle **E**, with its rather gaunt, ruined keep. Most of what can be seen dates from the 16th century, but there is some earlier stonework visible in the inner courtyard. An avenue of trees leads up to the main road through the town.

5 SANQUHAR TO WANLOCKHEAD

via Cogshead   *8 miles (13 km)*

This is a short section, but those who have completed the last stretch in one go will probably welcome the rest, and for others it allows time to explore the remains at Wanlockhead. Leaving the path from the castle, turn left onto the road into Sanquhar **77**. The town itself has a number of interesting features, including a post office that has been in business since 1738. Turn right up the road between the church and the garage **78**, go under the railway and keep following the road round until it

The gaunt ruins of Sanquhar Castle stand at the edge of the town above the River Nith.

becomes a track heading uphill through a patchwork of fields bordered by stone walls – the track's name spells out its main use, Cow's Wynd. Where the main track swings round to the right **79** carry straight on along the grassy path, which is quite indistinct but which follows the line of the wall, heading for a strip of conifers. Walk straight on through the woods and continue on the same line on the other side until the path turns left to go downhill towards the signpost at the edge of the woods **80**.

Turn right onto the road, and where the road divides, turn right again by the burn running in a deep gully. The Way soon divides again **81** and turns left on a path that heads towards the hills. At the edge of the woodland turn left onto a narrow path that has been built up across an area of boggy moor. Go round a small pool to head for the ladder stile and then strike straight across the moor, continuing on the same line when the built-up path ends. Head straight up the steep hillside – 'a good grunt' as one passing walker described it – following the line of the fence. At the end of the sharp climb there is an excuse to pause and admire the view down over the pattern of fields laid out between the folds of the hills. Cross a stile and continue following the line of the fence and eventually the path becomes hard and stony. Crossing another stile, the way rounds the shoulder of the hill, passing above a deep, conifer-lined cleft. Now the path runs down along the side of the valley heading for the edge of the plantation. At the bottom of the hill, the path swings round to a stile beyond which it joins a path through the forest. It passes through a neck of woodland and here the Way divides **82**. The old route keeps to forest roads for a long meander round the hills. For a far better, more open route – but one which involves a little more climbing – take a short cut over the hills. This, the recommended route, is the one described here.

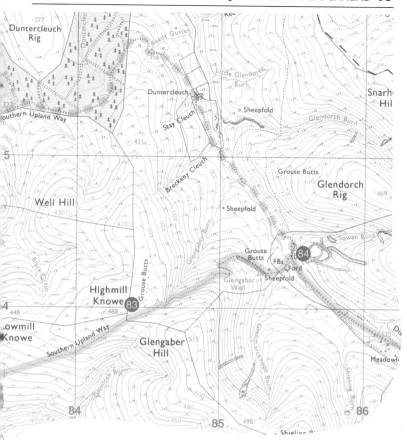

Turn right at the stile by the farm gate to climb the hill. At the wall turn left, still heading uphill, and once over the next stile turn right towards the end of the wooden fence. Cross the footbridge over a little gully, head for the next bridge, and then head for the stile by the gate. Now a clear stony path leads straight over the moor, still climbing slightly, but offering a wonderful airy situation. At the top of the hill **83** continue on the path running at an angle away from the fence, and going downhill. Down below, the scarred slopes of the lead-mining area of Wanlockhead come into view, while in the distance the radar domes and telecommunications masts mark the top of the Lowther Hills. At the bottom of the hill is a jumbled-up area of old smelt mills and spoil heaps. Cross the footbridge **84** and turn right onto the main track down the valley – those who have taken the long way round rejoin the route at this point. All along the way there are reminders of some three centuries of mining for lead and for smaller quantities of silver and gold. By one complex, with a piece of drive shafting still in place, an adit can be seen diving into the heart of the hill. The road passes old miners' cottages and the cemetery, where many headstones tell tales of fatal accidents. Just before the next row of cottages **85**, the Way turns to the right passing the remains of an 1845 smelt mill. It then turns right and immediately left onto an old tramway or waggonway along which horses once pulled loaded trucks. This area to the left is rich in industrial remains including the preserved beam engine (see p.27).

The path eventually emerges by the excellent museum, which is well worth a visit – and even those with no interest in industrial history might welcome a break at the museum cafe. There is a great deal to see in Wanlockhead, including the little library established by the miners in 1756.

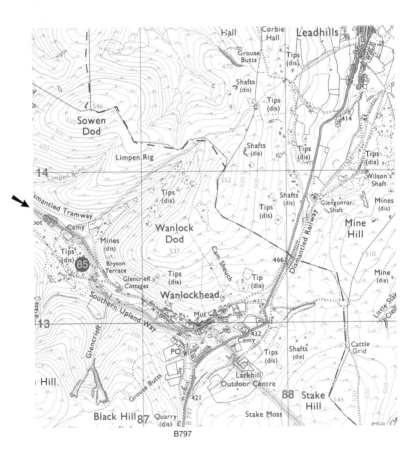

The scarred hillside dominates the old lead mining area of Wanlockhead, and tracks have been relaid on one of the mine tramways.

6 WANLOCKHEAD TO BEATTOCK

via Daer Reservoir   *20 miles (32 km)*

The short section is followed by a far longer one that begins with a walk to the highest point on the Southern Upland Way. It starts with a climb up the wooden steps by the museum entrance and then continues on to the cluster of huts that was once the Larkhill Outdoor Centre. Here an old signal **A** announces that you have arrived at the track of the short-lived Leadhills and Wanlockhead Light Railway, opened in 1902 and closed in 1938, but boasting for a time the highest station on a conventional railway in Britain. The route crosses the old line and continues uphill, emerging among heather moorland. Looking back, one can see how comfortably Wanlockhead snuggles in among the hills, while up ahead the 'golf balls' of the Civil Aviation radar system indicate the still-distant summit. The path levels out briefly to give a view of the reservoir to the right. Crossing a gully on a footbridge the long climb now begins. At the road turn right, then, as it begins to turn in an extravagant bend, abandon it again for a

Beam pump and miners' cottages at Wanlockhead.

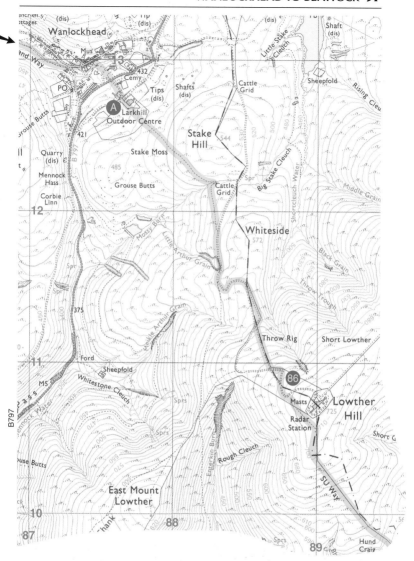

shorter, steeper walk through the heather. The road reappears but the path goes straight on over to a grassy path beside the fence, and the zigzagging road is crossed yet again. All the time the view is opening out, and one can look back over the ranges of hills already crossed. Nearing the top of the hill, just below the golf balls **86**, turn right onto the road and then as it heads away again carry straight on along the grassy track, leaving the radar installation to the left.

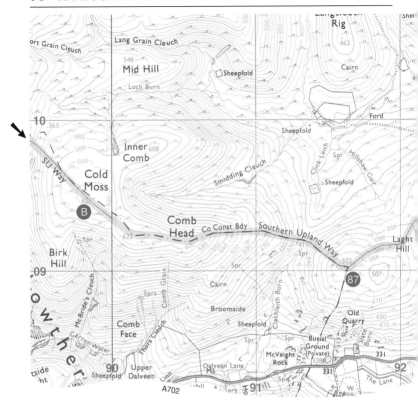

Cross a stile and head past a small hut. The path contours the hill, above a deep valley where bluff hills fold, as though the hill had been taken in a giant's hand and crumpled like paper. From this point, cross the stile and the way turns right towards gentler slopes. The Way soon begins to go steeply downhill, but it is clear that this is only a temporary reprieve, before it goes just as steeply uphill again. It is all quite demanding, but there is ample reward in terms of exhilarating scenery. From the top of the next hill **B** there are contrasting views, with gentle slopes to the left and more rugged hills to the right. There is excellent walking now along the rounded ridge, before plunging down again and like a roller coaster climbing straight up again. At the top of the next hill, at the wall junction **87** turn left. Now there is an altogether gentler descent and the route becomes a little stony path winding through the heather. It comes down to a gate and then runs parallel to the wall, and a familiar sight soon appears in the form of a wide belt of conifers. Cross a stile and come down to the main road **88** and turn left.

Walk beside the road, cross the river and turn right, not over the stile but through the gate next to it **89**. Cross the field on a diagonal heading for a stile by a wooden gate, and follow the fence round towards the river. Cross the river on a small footbridge by a little weir and continue alongside the river past an area of felled woodland. Just after the big bend in the river, turn right to head down the broad fire break. At the broad track **90** turn right through an area of dark, dense brooding forest. At the large clearing where the track divides, continue straight on. Leave the forest by the stile next to the gate and continue on the obvious track that soon swings to the left. There is a brief interlude where the trees are completely cleared and there are wide views over the moorland, before the next conifer plantation is reached. For a while, however, the track skirts the edge of the forest and there is a chance to look back at the golf balls on Lowther Hill.

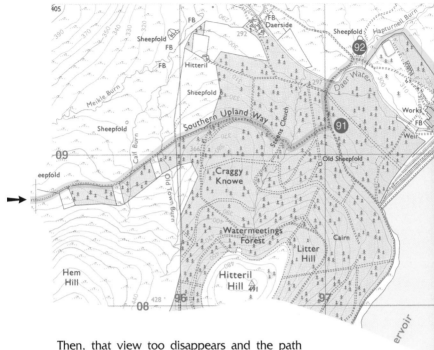

Then, that view too disappears and the path
plunges back into dense woodland where unseen
pheasants call harshly to each other. The path runs
steadily downhill, and there is a brief opening out at a felled area and
a little gurgling burn offers diversion. At the road **91** turn left, and continue down to cross the attractive Daer Water. Up ahead are the waterworks and a row of cottages that mark the head of the Daer Reservoir.

As the road divides **92** turn right, then, by the plaque announcing
that the reservoir was opened by the Queen in 1956, turn left to follow
the fence round to the right behind the strip of conifers. This is very
heavy going through wet ground and great clumps of coarse grass –
made all the harder by knowing that there is a private road running in
front of the houses! As the tussocks end, head for a ladder stile. As the
path clears the woodland, the reservoir with its massive dam quickly
comes into view. Turn left **93** to follow the path uphill beside the wall.
This is a good long slog, and one of those irritating climbs where you
keep thinking the top is in sight only to breast the rise and discover the
hillside still going relentlessly upwards. The gradient finally begins to
ease and the actual summit comes into view. The reward for hard work
comes at the summit **C** from where it is possible to see a distant gleam
of water at the Solway Firth and the dark hills of the Lakeland Fells.

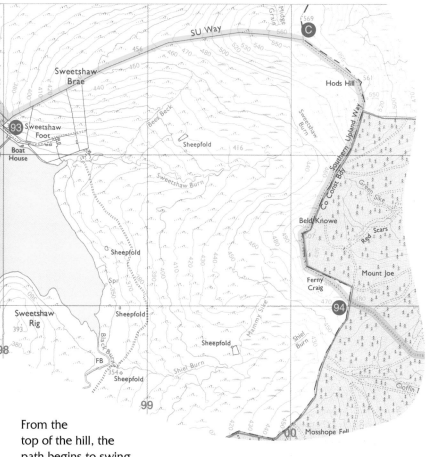

From the
top of the hill, the
path begins to swing
down to the right, still following the
fence. This is a very Duke-of-York section of the Way, for whenever
you march down a hill you can be certain that you are going to march
up it again – and that is precisely what happens, up to another good
viewpoint. The path now continues by the fence and runs beside the
forest that will dominate the next section of the walk. At the top of
this hill, follow the wall round to the left, but where the wall turns
sharp left continue straight on for another 70 yards and then turn onto
the green track through paler clumps to head for the obvious break in
the trees **94**. This cuts a broad avenue downhill through the trees,
allowing the walker to continue to enjoy the view up ahead. There is
also a chance to see as well as hear the woodland birds, notably
thrush, robin and chaffinch. A little burn in a deep gully appears, and

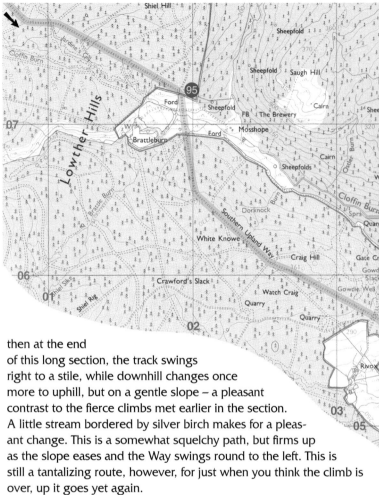

then at the end
of this long section, the track swings
right to a stile, while downhill changes once
more to uphill, but on a gentle slope – a pleasant
contrast to the fierce climbs met earlier in the section.
A little stream bordered by silver birch makes for a pleasant change. This is a somewhat squelchy path, but firms up
as the slope eases and the Way swings round to the left. This is
still a tantalizing route, however, for just when you think the climb is
over, up it goes yet again.

At the top of the rise, a new noise is heard that is happily rarely
present on the Way, the noise of heavy traffic drifting up from the
A74. The route now follows a switchback of a ridge, with trees clos-
ing off the view, but topping the rise there is at least an encouraging
view of a long downhill walk. At the bottom of the hill **95** cross the
stile, cross over forest tracks and continue in the same direction.
Down in the valley there are occasional glimpses of farmhouses
again. Cross the stream by the footbridge or the ford. Eventually, after
a good deal more forest walking, a ladder stile **96** leads to an open
space, which is crossed to an obvious break in the next forest section
opposite. It comes as something of a surprise to come across a farm

here, isolated in the middle of such a vast area of forest – and a little rocky knoll with a topping of stunted trees is a reminder of what all of this area was like not so very long ago. Cross the footbridge, which has a memorial to Lance Corporal Foy, who was killed in a motor accident. The path wanders through an area of brackish, weedy pools, before turning back into the forest **97**.

The broad forest track is closed in to either side, with very little variety to the view until it reaches a clearing where it dives off

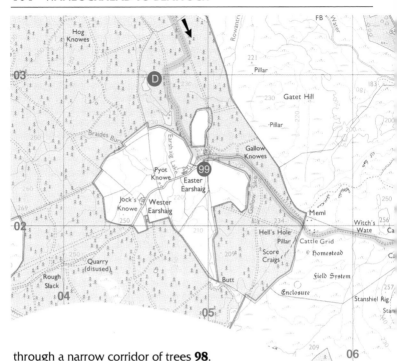

through a narrow corridor of trees **98**.
This leads down to an attractive area **D** where a
small loch sits amid grassy banks bright with flowers and sur
rounded by tall pines. A notice board gives information about the
Way and the history of transport in the area. Leave the forest by the
wooden gate and continue straight down to the road **99** and turn left.
This road now leads all the way down to Beattock. The Moffat Forest
has been left and in its place is a rock-strewn upland. Beattock Hill **E**
was ringed with a defence ditch and rampart by Iron Age settlers, but
it now serves as a council rubbish tip. One can see the effort farmers
have made to clear the land. Many of the stones have gone to build
the field walls, while the rest have been gathered together in great
heaps. The main road now comes into view with the town of Moffat
beyond it, and the next range of hills can be seen in the distance. This
valley holds a vast rabbit population, who can be seen dashing furi-
ously around in every field. The road crosses over the main
London–Glasgow railway and passes a farm with an odd little circular
building with a conical roof. This was originally a horse-mill. The ani-
mals would endlessly trudge on a circular track to turn the mill, which
was geared to a threshing machine. The road ends at the junction
near the river with the Beattock Hotel and camp site opposite **F**.

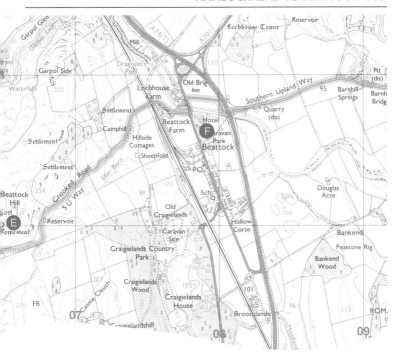

Sheep graze the hillside above Beattock.

7 BEATTOCK TO ST MARY'S LOCH

via Ettrick Head   *21 miles (33 km)*

At the Beattock road junction **100** turn left, cross the bridge and turn right onto the path that heads towards the main road. It makes its way down an avenue of beech before turning right by the road to the river and passing under the busy and noisy A74 **101**. The route now becomes a gentle stroll down country lanes, and the rabbits, no longer content with just fields, hop cheekily around through everyone's gardens. Indeed, even the local deer are no respecters of property rights and may be spotted heading for a sapling breakfast. Up in

The attractive riverside walk along Moffat Water.

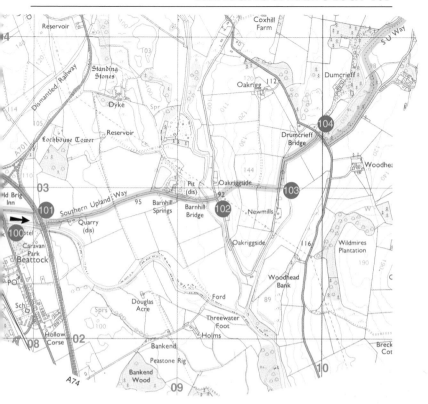

the beech trees, inhabitants of a rookery exchange raucous gossip. The river is crossed on an odd metal-decked bridge and the road arrives at a T-junction **102**. Cross the ladder stile opposite and turn slightly left to take a short cut over the hill. At the top go straight down again, following the wall, and turn left to rejoin the road **103**.

This is a quiet road overhung by trees, with nothing to disturb the peace but the splash and rush of the river alongside. At the road junction **104** turn right to cross the bridge with a sight of a handsome house, once the home of the great road engineer John Loudon Macadam, enjoying a splendid situation. Turn immediately left up the road beside the wood and look for a ladder stile to cross for a footpath through the trees, a fine mixture of birch, native pine and beech, which provide a crunchy footpath of nuts. The path swings away from the road to head down towards the river and an equally pleasant walk along the bank. The attractive mixture of river, meadows and broadleaved woodland is quite unlike anything else met along the Way.

Cross straight over the road and continue on the riverside track. The crumbling remains of Cornal Tower **A** can be seen among the trees as the path swings round to the right beside a long strip of conifers.

We are now back with more familiar Southern Upland territory as the track climbs steadily then doubles back through a sharp bend to head towards a forest plantation. The peace of this area is likely to be disturbed at any time by very low-flying RAF jets. The track is still steadily climbing, with a fringe of broad-leaved trees beside the little stream, contrasting with the dark spruce. It crosses the stream with its flowery banks, and looking back one can still see the distant domes on Lowther Hill. Then at the next stile the trees close in on both sides. As the track begins to level, gaps appear but offer little more than a view of more forested hills. More variety appears when a burn that has been chortling cheerfully out of sight finally puts in an appearance. Where the track divides **105**, continue on the main track to cross the stream. At the top of the hill a neat little sign announces that you have arrived at lonely Hope Cottage, and as another track joins in from the left, the Way starts heading downhill. Pools by the trackside are perfectly clear, in contrast with the peaty darkness of the moors.

The Way ahead appears to be blocked by an alarmingly steep-sided hill, but the track swings round to the right to pass round the

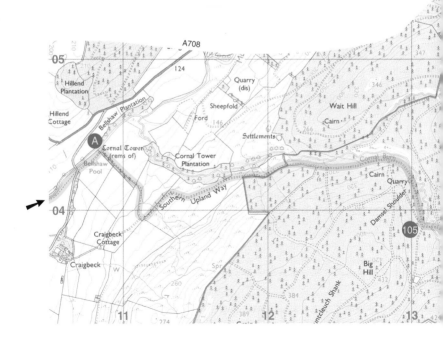

foot of it. Then, as the path doubles back **106**, turn left onto the grassy path beside the stream. This undoubtedly makes a pleasant change, though there is a great deal of hopping from stone to stone as the path crosses and recrosses the water. Gradually, the trees begin to thin out to reveal heather-covered hillsides, and the whole walk suddenly becomes much more dramatic. Tongues of scree lick down the hill and clumps of heather line the path: all very delightful, if rather squelchy underfoot. Crossing a stile with a wire fence to the left, continue along the foot of the hill and a splendid view unfolds **B** of craggy hills rising above a narrow gorge, down which a waterfall tumbles. The path turns away from the gorge off to the hill on the right. It rounds the shoulder as a narrow path clinging to the steep slope as it makes its way back to the gully where spume from the falls flies up above the rim.

The path now levels out and continues creeping round the rocky hillside before crossing the burn on a footbridge and heading for the little knoll opposite. It is worth pausing to turn back to enjoy another look at this wild scene. The path drops down into a hollow and then heads off towards the next batch of forest up ahead.

A stile in a wire fence **C** marks Ettrick Head and an important boundary, not just because Dumfries and Galloway are being left behind and the Borders region is beginning, but because this is a watershed and streams and rivers will now be flowing towards the east. The path heads into the forest and turns right onto a wide track **107**. This is good, firm going and comparatively open, so there are wide views across the tree-covered hills. The route ahead can be seen heading right down to the valley floor. It is all very pleasant, with large gaps in the forest and a mountain stream for company. Once down in the fertile valley, farms begin to appear again with some regularity, and the track swings round to cross Ettrick Water at the well-maintained Over Phawhope bothy **D** – someone has even planted flowers by the door.

Once over the bridge, the track continues following the line of the river. The scenery has changed yet again, the craggy slopes replaced by more softly moulded hills. The track passes a large farmhouse, climbs gently uphill and continues as a metalled road that will be followed for the next 5 miles (8 km). The road runs fairly straight, perched above the river, apart from a U-turn as it crosses a stream rushing down from the hills. All the time what had seemed, at first, no

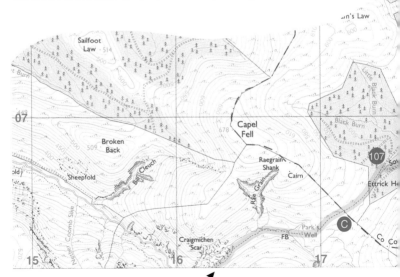

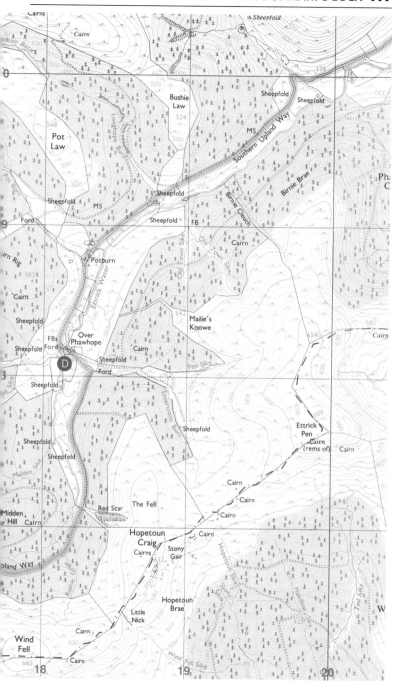

more than a hill stream is gathering strength and taking on the character of a spectacularly swift river. Farms begin to appear with great regularity. Nether Phawhope **E** is notable for its lovely setting above a little rocky gully bordered by pine, and also for the superb workmanship displayed in its circular drystone sheepfolds. The road runs along beside the river for a while, and when it is not dashing down the rapids, one can admire the vari-coloured stones on the bed, a mixture of greys, greens and soft yellows. Gradually, the hills begin to close in up ahead. The road leaves the river by an area of flat fields, with a farmhouse beyond. Here the road
walking ends **108**.

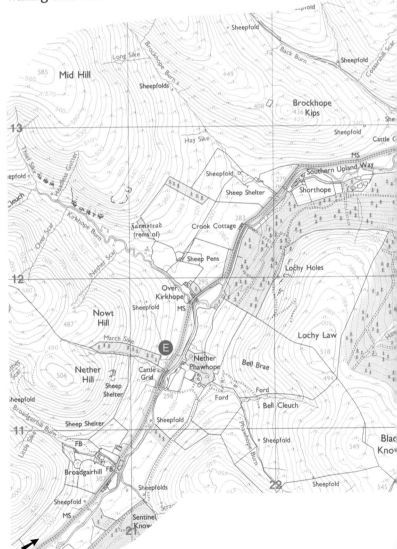

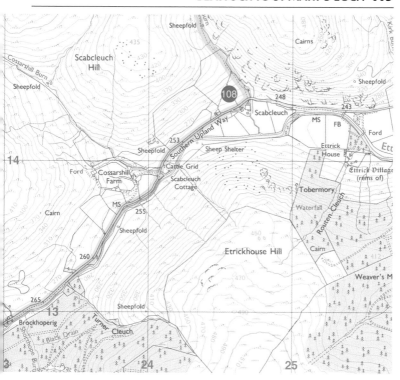

St Mary's Loch with its splendid background of hills.

Turn left opposite the farmhouse over a stone stile and begin heading uphill. It is a stiff little climb to a second stile in the corner of the field by the gully, which the walk runs up alongside. There is a sense of exhilaration at being back in rough country, with a rock-strewn hill to one side and the stream descending steeply through a succession of falls. Gully and path keep company until the way opens out into a great moorland plateau, resounding with curlew cries. A few crows try to join the singing contest, but come a poor second.

As the stream dwindles away, the route ahead appears as a pale, stony path heading across the moor, towards the obvious gap in the low hills. There is a great air of solitude and stillness here, an area of open landscape and wide sky. The path briefly follows the line of a fence, but soon turns away as a raised track, kept dry by drainage ditches to either side. Once a stile is crossed, the path runs along the contour on the flank of Peniestone Knowe, with a long, scooped-out valley down below. It continues along to the end of the ridge **109** then swings sharply off to the right to go steeply downhill, crossing a small gully. A gleam of water on the left is Loch of the Lowes, a sign that the end of the section is not too far away. The path heads for the ruined farmhouse in the valley. Turn left at the ruins **110** onto the main track that runs across the cattle grid and swings right to circle the hill. This is a rough farm track that descends steadily, past a

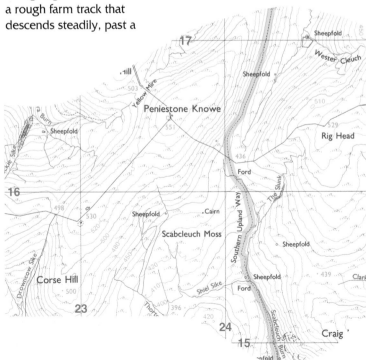

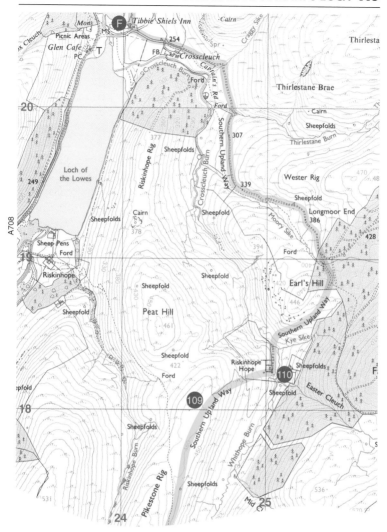

border of green slate poking through the hill. Eventually, it turns far enough round for St Mary's Loch at last to come into view. It heads straight down now to a popular resting place, Tibbie Shiels Inn **F**. Tibbie was a mole-catcher's wife who started the inn when her husband died in 1824. She continued to run it until her death in 1878 at the age of 96, and Tibbie Shiels Inn it remains. It is also the spot where the Southern Upland Way was officially inaugurated in 1984.

Tibbie Shiels Inn by St Mary's Loch. It was here that the Southern Upland Way w

fficially inaugurated.

8 ST MARY'S LOCH TO TRAQUAIR

via Dryhope   *12 miles (19 km)*

After two fairly tough sections, this offers something of a breather. The Way goes right past Tibbie Shiels, then goes through the grounds of the sailing club to join the lochside path. This is a busy spot, particularly at weekends, when the sailing fraternity are joined by paragliders launching themselves from the surrounding hills. The path follows the shoreline quite closely all the way to the far end. It wanders across fields that slope steeply to the water's edge, past a fine stand of tall pine, before the plantation appears to blanket the hillside. New plantings of broad-leaved trees at the fringe should add variety once they have matured. The path now comes right down to the water's edge, then, as a wall bars the way, turns uphill again to

follow a higher level for a short while, but soon returns again – like a small child dipping its toes in the cold water, dashing away and coming back for more. At the farm entrance **111** the path gives way to a forest track, but even though the trees come right down to the water, there are still views over the loch.

At the end of the loch **112** cross the bridge, then turn immediately right over the stile to follow the path along the river bank. Sheep graze peacefully beside the gently flowing stream. At the next stile, head diagonally across the field towards the gate. Up ahead is the dramatic outline of Dryhope Tower **A**. Cross the road and the stile on the other side to continue in the same direction up the farm track, which becomes a grassy track beside the wall. Closer up, one can see what an uncompromising defensive building the tower is, making no concessions to luxury or even basic comfort. Leaving the field, turn right onto the track that heads up towards the gap in the hills. Down below, a mountain stream rushes along between banks of heather, and a little rocky gorge with a waterfall soon comes into view. Shortly after, the fence ends and the track starts to swing to the left **113**. Turn right onto the grassy path.

As Southern Upland hill climbs go, this is a very gentle affair up to the saddle between the hills, where it turns towards the summit on the right and a view back to St Mary's Loch. The Way then turns left to go down the ridge to cross a number of boggy hill streams on a succession of footbridges. The path swings round the foot of South Hawkshaw Rig, making for very pleasant walking in this bowl of hills. Now the path swings right and then left before dropping down to cross the tree-lined burn. The spoil heaps on the hillside to the right mark the site of an old gold mine. Once over the stream head up the wooden steps and continue in the same direction to join the track that swings down towards a farmhouse and cottage. Cross the broad Douglas Burn and head for the point where the tracks meet by the crumbling remains of Blackhouse Tower **B**. Cross the stile, turn right and then left to walk in front of the house and through the farmyard to take the track that leads up into the forest. The initial steepness of the climb is greatly helped by the spring and bounce of the turf, and in any case it soon eases off. As the forest closes in, there is another view back to the loch. The path continues to climb as it heads through the trees, and is still going uphill when it reaches the far side, where there is the appealing sight of a great expanse of open moor.

The open scenery of the Hawkshaw Rigs above St Mary's Loch.

The hard track now gives way to softer walking on grass, but, necessarily, the Way then becomes less distinct. The general direction remains the same, and although there are no obvious landmarks, there are well-placed waymarkers. As it heads downhill the Way becomes decidedly clearer and eventually an obvious track emerges that swings round to the right. It climbs the hillside towards a gate with a marker post beyond. At the top of the rise **114** the path turns left towards a dark, heather-covered hill. Once the Way begins to descend, a definite landmark appears in the shape of a prominent clump of conifers, and soon a stile by a gate can be spotted. A slightly sunken path winds through the heather, and the town of Innerleithen comes into view down in the valley. The going is comfortable, the views are superb and altogether this is a most exhilarating section of moorland walking.

Leaving the moor by the stile, the path heads across a field towards the end of the tongue of conifer licking up the hill. Crossing the stile at the end of the woods **115**, continue downhill by a series of marker posts, still heading towards Innerleithen. Eventually, head to the gate by a junction of stone walls and follow the wall down through an area of gorse bushes. This leads directly to a footpath, with conifers to one side and gorse to the other, that swoops down to a farm track and a parade of beech that ends at the road **116**. Turn left at the road past the neat little 18th-century church with

B709

an external staircase that leads straight into a gallery. Beyond it is handsome Kirkbridge House with a fine, walled garden. It is very noticeable how much more prosperous everything seems here in the fertile valley than in the bare uplands. The road now leads straight on to Traquair, which comes into view beyond the bridge. Over on the right is the little village school, on an idyllic hillside site, surrounded by trees and fields. This section ends at a crossroads **117**, where there is a choice on offer. The Way turns right up the road marked 'No Through Road', but those with time and energy to spare should certainly walk the extra half mile to the left in order to visit Traquair House to sample its architecture and its history – not to mention the products of its brewery.

Traquair and the Tweed Valley, with the surrounding hills patched by woodland.

9 TRAQUAIR TO MELROSE

via Yair Bridge and Galashiels   *16½ miles (26 km)*

Leaving Traquair, start out on the road but as it turns to the right towards the school continue straight on along the track. There is a brisk climb through a narrow band of conifers followed by a short open interlude, before the tracks turn to the left towards a great mass of forest. The stony path climbs up into the trees, crosses a broad forest track and marches relentlessly on up the hill, shut in by deep, dark forest. Eventually, the trees clear for a glimpse of the hills to the left, and as the Way climbs so the views broaden. The heather-covered hill of Minch Moor appears, and those who want a spectacular view point can walk up to the top. Others can pause by the little spring emerging from the Cheese Well **A**. This owes its odd name to the days when this was a drove road and passers-by would leave a little offering of cheese to placate the wee folk.

The Way now skirts the summit and begins to head downhill. The woodland has a lively bird population, and this is one spot where there is a chance of seeing short-eared owls. As the path becomes grassier, the shapely peaks of the Eildon Hills pop up over the horizon and will continue to put in an appearance from time to time until the section ends at Melrose at their foot. The downhill route through the forest is altogether airier than the uphill, with wide gaps in the trees and plenty of opportunity to enjoy the heather-covered hills. Topping a rise, the trees retreat and give way to wide vistas and comfortable walking through roundly swelling hills clad in grass and heather – a wonderful, colourful scene when the heather is in bloom. At the edge of the woods **118** the path divides and the Way heads left towards the summit

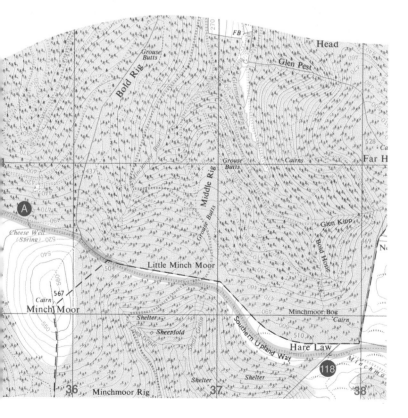

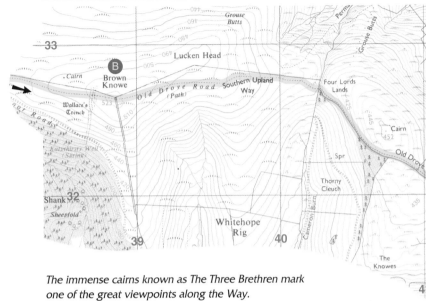

The immense cairns known as *The Three Brethren* mark
one of the great viewpoints along the Way.

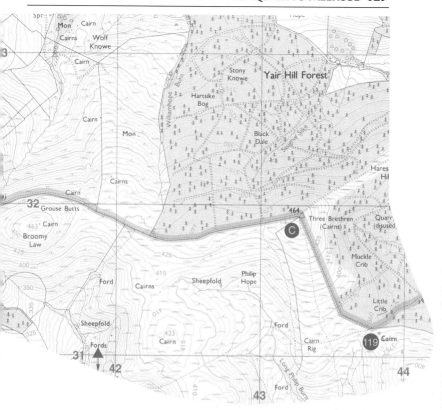

of the rounded hill. This is a good, steady climb on soft turf with varied views to enjoy and it seems no time at all before the summit cairn is reached **B**. Here is a complete panorama, a 360° sweep round the best of Southern Upland scenery. The Way continues by crossing a stile, still keeping to the old drove road.

The route heads downhill past a small knot of pines, and then goes uphill beside the tree-lined wall. Stones give way to a grassy path as the Way skirts the flanks of Broomy Law, heading for the prominent cairns known as the Three Brethren. This is magnificent country, the swell of the hills and the dip of the valley as regular as a slowly heaving sea. A line of grouse butts is crossed, rather like soldiers' dug-outs, and just beyond that a path to the right gives access to a youth hostel. The main route leads on to the plantation and runs along the side of the woods to the cairns **C**. They are remarkable examples of what can be built without the benefit of cement or mortar. Here, the path turns right to go very steeply downhill. The path goes through a fence **119** and then turns left into the woods on a pleasant little downhill walk on

The Way below the Cheese Well passing through dense forest but with a prospect

en hill walking up ahead.

a carpet of pine needles. It crosses a broad forest road and continues straight on as a narrow path through the trees. It swings left towards a wider forest track by a clearing, but crosses over it to follow a hollow that swings off to the right **120**. This leads through an area of felled trees, with a small stream trickling along to the right. The path then crosses a little burn running through a deep cleft and emerges in an area of mixed woodland with open fields to the side. It plunges briefly into the dense woods, but soon re-emerges to follow the line of the field wall. This provides a pleasant contrast to the dominant theme of spruce plantations, for here the mixed woods are dominated by beech interspersed with great clumps of rhododendra. The grey slate roof of a house appears to mark the end of the forest walk.

On reaching the road **121** with a view of the fine 18th-century House of Yair, turn right along the bank of the broad River Tweed and head for the three-arched bridge **122** with its prominent cut waters, dividing the river that rushes past in a series of rapids. Cross the bridge and follow the road round to the left, then immediately beyond the row of cottages turn right onto the farm track. This is another area with a vast rabbit population

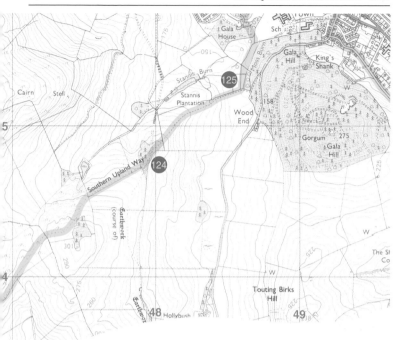

hopping in and out of the farm buildings. Walk up beside the attractive area of broad-leaved woodland and cross straight over the tree-lined avenue to continue uphill on the track. The path then swings right to cut through a strip of woodland and in the next field, where the track divides **123**, turn to the right to continue uphill towards the gap in the woods. A cottage on the right enjoys spectacular views and the surrounding fields look as if their prominent bumps and lumps have been treated with stone plaster, though the patches are simply the stones cleared from the land. Once through the woods, the path continues along the line of the wall and eventually heads off towards a marker post to the left of the next copse. The Way is not very distinct at this point, but it passes through a farm gate after which a stone stile soon comes into view. Once over this stile, carry on straight ahead and the next objective, the town of Galashiels, comes into sight. Now the path turns right and heads downhill to a stile and follows the wall down to a patch of woodland **124**. Take the path through the beech wood and then head diagonally down towards the wall on the left.

The rougher country is now left behind for richer farmland. The path joins the wall near the edge of the wood. At this point **125** the Way has been rerouted recently to provide better access to the facilities of Galashiels. Turn left to follow the path round the edge of the wood, which is full of mature oak, beech and birch. Continue on round the back of the large, modern school and then turn left through a mass of rhododendra, cross a footbridge at the edge of a pond and continue round to pass in front of the school. The path now emerges into Galashiels, a town that prospered on its many woollen mills. Those carrying straight on along the Way without a break should turn right through the playground area to the church with its tall, elaborately carved sandstone steeple **126**. At the road turn right and where it swings right turn left down Barr Road, which is lined by a mixture of modern houses and older stone villas. Soon the houses begin to thin out and the road peters out into a tree-lined footpath circling the foot of Gala Hill. Suddenly, it is all quite rural again, and the trees that send knotted roots out across the path shield walkers from the noise of traffic in the valley. The path ends by a memorial to Roger Quinn, who described the view of 'Scotland's Eden' – some time before the gas works and the industrial estate were completed!

The Way continues along the line of the wall and there is a first sight of Sir Walter Scott's Abbotsford **D** in its magnificent setting beside the river with a backdrop of hills. The route continues over farmland to the corner of a field **127** where it doubles back towards

The attractive grassland of Hog Hill, with the distinctive and shapely Eildon Hills in the distance.

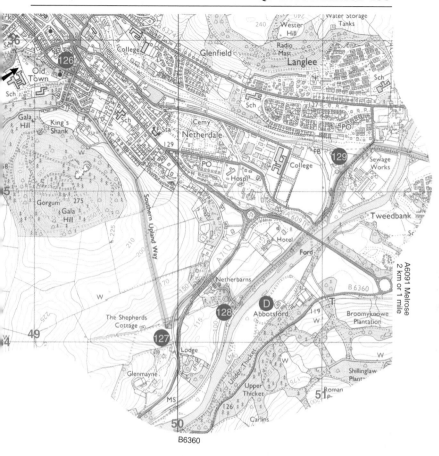

B6360

the large stone house and continues on down to the road. Turn right and immediately left to take the steps down to the busy main road. Cross over and take the dead-end road opposite between the farm and the cottages. Follow the road down to the bottom of the hill **128** and turn left onto the riverside path by the Tweed. The air here is heavy with the scent of wild garlic, martins swoop and dive over the water and Abbotsford appears in its full baronial splendour. A curiously modern note was struck by a fisherman expertly casting his fly while chatting on his mobile phone. It is a glorious riverscape, the water running fast and deep; the path now climbing up through the trees and now dropping back to the water's edge.

The idyll is temporarily broken as the path passes beneath the new concrete girder bridge, where it joins the road past the gas works to turn right to cross a tributary stream **129** and continues straight on up the road. Where the power lines cross the road, turn right to join a metalled track. This is a footpath and cycle track created out of the track bed of the old North British railway line that survived until 1969. It crosses the river on a high viaduct and then heads off on what appears as a wholly countrified route, though an occasional glimpse of roofs shows that it is never far from the urban areas. It is altogether a splendid example of the re-use of old railways as a quite different type of transport amenity. Where the path meets the road **130**, continue straight on towards the Barbour factory, then turn off the approach road, cross a stile and continue along the path beside the river. This is an attractive riverside walk over fields studded with mature trees, and which is, not surprisingly, very popular with strolling locals. As the bank steepens up ahead, the path turns away from the river briefly to join the road at the edge of Melrose. Then, almost immediately it turns again to a footpath that climbs gently to the river bank. There is a fine view down to the river, which tumbles down over a weir with a delicate suspension bridge just beyond. It arrives at an area of public gardens, the classically restrained church of 1810 and a bowling green **131**. For those stopping at Melrose, whether to admire the magnificent abbey remains, to pay homage at the birthplace of seven-a-side Rugby, or simply to enjoy a rest and a pint, this is the spot to turn off for the town. The rest should continue on the riverside path to

the suspension bridge **E**.

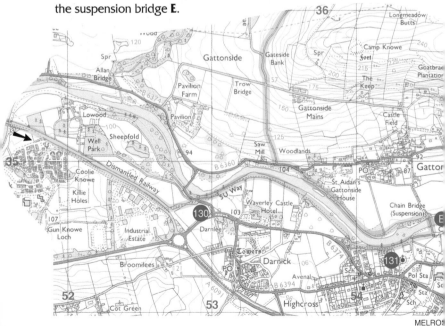

Rich red stone and elaborate carving combine to create the unique beauty of Melrose Abbey, magnificent even in ruins.

The robust yet elegant road bridge that takes the Way across the turbulent Tweed at Ya

10 MELROSE TO LONGFORMACUS

via Lauder and Twin Law   *25 miles (40 km)*

This section starts at the suspension bridge, a testimony to the quality of 19th-century engineering, built in 1826 and only repaired a century later. It has castellated towers in the popular Gothic style to give suitable dignity. Cross the bridge, turn left and head back up the river, with a view across to the section already walked. The path enters an area of woodland with a grand mansion above it and then turns to join the road. Turn left to continue in the same direction for a short way, then at the brow of the hill **132** turn right onto the tree-lined track. At the end of a quite steep little climb, the track arrives at a road junction and continues straight on along the road opposite. Then, where the road turns sharply left **133**, continue straight on along the farm track lined with beech.

This hill crossing is unlike others met along the Way in that it never reaches a height where fields are left behind. There are changes, however, *en route*: the long, lush grass of the valley gives way to shorter, wirier tufts at the top of the climb, but it remains a land of neat field divisions. The track becomes rock strewn, and soon narrows down to a path.

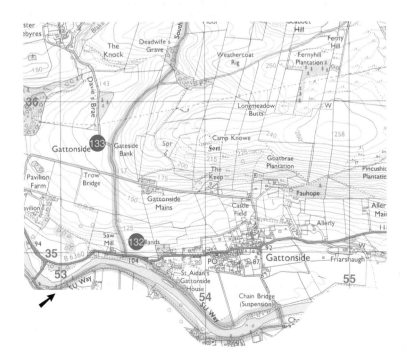

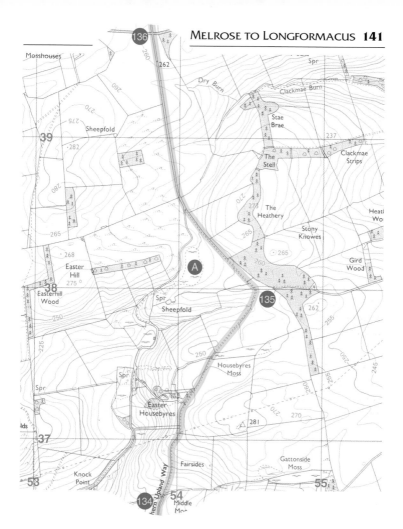

Interest along the way is provided by a rowdy rookery in a copse and by views back over Melrose and the Eildon Hills, and colour is added by gorse and hawthorn. At the end of the path **134** go straight on across the next field, keeping the wall on the left, the Way still brightened by gorse and heather overlooked by tall pine. At the top of the hill the Way finally levels out as it passes the farm, with its cluster of trees. The track continues across the fields to a large patch of woodland where it turns left **135** past the tip of the woods. Cross a stile and continue following the contours of the hill to head for a knoll with a clump of trees. The marshy land to the left **A** is a popular gathering place for gulls, and although there are patches of moorland, much of the land has been cleared and walled off. The track now switchbacks its way down to the road **136**.

The old Tolbooth in the centre of Lauder.

Cross the road and continue along the track opposite. Vistas of hills that have featured all the way along the walk now give way to views over altogether gentler farmland. This is a firm track running between stone walls and patches of gorse towards a farm with a factory-like chimney, indicating that at one time it used steam power for threshing. Join the road at the end of the long strip of woodland **137** and continue in the same direction along the road opposite. Just beyond the houses **138** turn left past the trees and follow the wall along below the trig point. This is a comparatively noisy part of the walk: first there is the crackle and hiss of power lines, then another wood full of raucous rooks. Where the lane ends at a stone stile, continue on in the same direction and as a change from hard tracks there is the

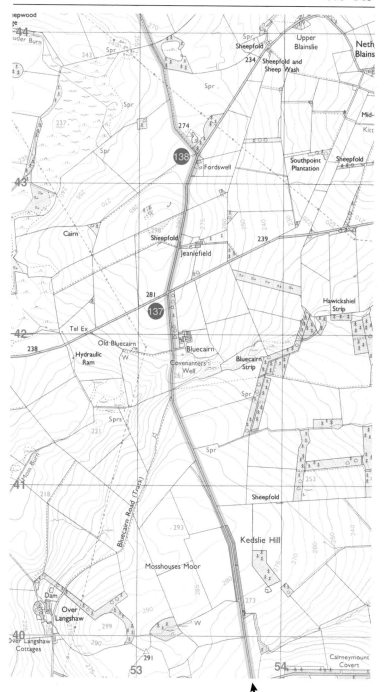

pleasure of walking on soft grass. The Way continues to follow the obvious line beside the wall, passing old farm buildings and skirting a small wood. The view from the top of the hill is still of a wide expanse of farmland, but there are signs of change up ahead.

Cross straight over the road **139** and continue to follow the edge of the wood. Now the path begins to go downhill and a steep-sided valley appears in front to block the way. Once over a ladder stile, turn away from the valley edge **140** where it descends almost vertically to a stream and head off to the right, aiming for the top of the little hill. The path now approaches the edge of the golf course, but keeps close to the rim of the attractive valley, passing an old quarry working and a small copse. Lauder comes into view, dominated by its 17th-century parish church with its impressive octagonal tower. The path runs alongside the golf course, and the remains of an old Iron Age hill fort **B**, its defensive earthworks reduced to a hazard for golfers. The path now heads straight downhill towards Lauder. At the road **141** turn left. At the church **142** the official route turns right down Factors Park, which seems a shame as the town centre is just a few yards ahead. Many walkers will understandably want to visit the town, and those who do should simply walk on down to the main road, where the Tolbooth looks out over the market place. The building has served as both prison and council chambers, suggesting a cynical view of the virtues of local government. Those making the detour should turn right and will rejoin the official route at the far end of Factors Park, which joins in at an acute angle on the right, and continue straight on down the main road.

Turn left past the step-gabled lodge **143** and onto the driveway to Thirlestane Castle **C**, which passes stables, grander than many country houses. Then, as it turns left, continue straight on across flat fields towards the river. There is ample evidence that the local mole catcher has been busy, as more than a hundred withered bodies are strung out along the fence. Cross the footbridge over the Leader Water **144** and turn left along the river bank as far as the fence, then turn uphill to follow the edge of the wood and then continue to follow round the edge of the next patch of woodland. From here there is a superb view of the castle, with its old medieval core given a new look by enthusiastically romantic restorers. At a broad forest track, turn left following the line of the fence and stay on the path as it turns right to head into the woods. It is a most pleasant walk along a ledge on the hillside, with a little stream trickling away down below.

Leave the woods by the gate **145** and turn right onto the track that skirts the woods. Cross over the road and carry straight on towards

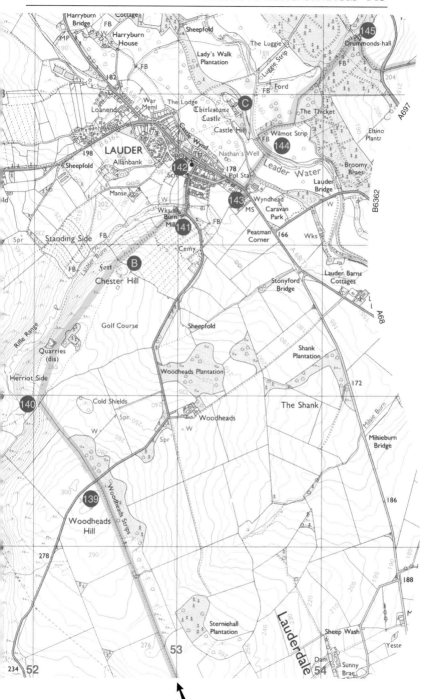

the curiously named Wanton Walls farm **146**. Turn left onto the metalled farm road to continue past the water-supply filter station, heading straight uphill towards the wood. From here there is a view back over Lauder and the whole valley. The path goes into the woods a little way, before turning right and coming out again. Turn left on leaving the woods, then left again by the stile and continue uphill following the wall at the edge of the woods. Once over the next stile **147** turn away from the wall for a post at the top of the hill. Out in the open now walking is easy on springy turf, while up ahead there is the fine prospect of a vast expanse of heather moorland. The path continues in the same direction towards a squared-off plantation. Leave the field by the stile to the left of the cattle grid, and carry on along the line of the wall.

The nature of the land goes through its now familiar change as the soft grass of the

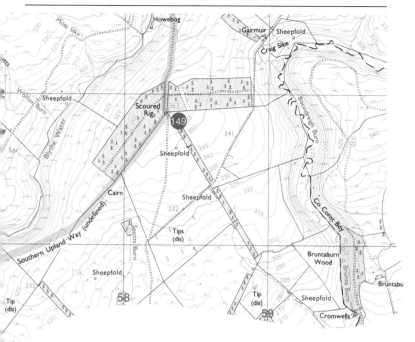

fields gives way to the coarse tufts of the moor. It remains, however, springy underfoot as the path twists and turns, still heading for the plantation. Topping the rise a more immediate objective comes into view, a little footbridge over the stream down in the valley. This is a comparatively recent deviation from the original route – the bridge was only built in 1993. Once over the bridge **148** turn diagonally left onto the rocky path up the opposite side of the valley, where the slope is so riddled with rabbit holes it looks as if it has been used as an artillery firing range. Once up the steep rise, turn slightly right to a gate just visible beyond a pile of stones. From here one can see how the little valley makes a clear division in the land, with heather moorland to one side and soft green turf and moss to the other. Once over the next stile aim for the right-hand side of the plantation that has been a landmark for so long. Watch out for a stile in the fence on the right, then cross it and carry straight on along the opposite side of the fence. The route keeps to the outside of the dense spruce wood: even the local pheasants seem to prefer to stroll the fields with the sheep rather than wander in its dark interior. Head for the broad break in the trees **149** and pass straight through the middle of the woods, back to the open moor.

The prospect changes once again, and now a solitary isolated farm tucked away in a hollow seems the only intrusion into an immense spread of moor. This is now the start also of a very large grouse-shooting estate. The path heads down towards the farm, then swings away to the right up the valley, to cross the first line of grouse butts **D**, rough horseshoes of dry-stone wall with turf topping where the guns wait for the birds to be driven towards them. This is an all-but-featureless – and shelterless – landscape matted with heather, beautiful on a fine day but merciless and bleak in bad weather. Where the track divides by the corner of a wire fence **150**, continue straight on. This is very much a walk for those who enjoy wild solitude and the tuneful company of lark and curlew. The heather seems to stretch from horizon to horizon, and there are views

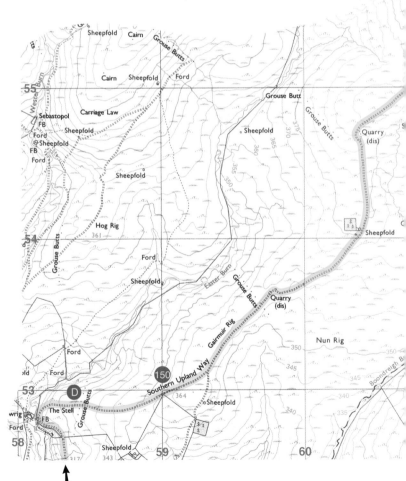

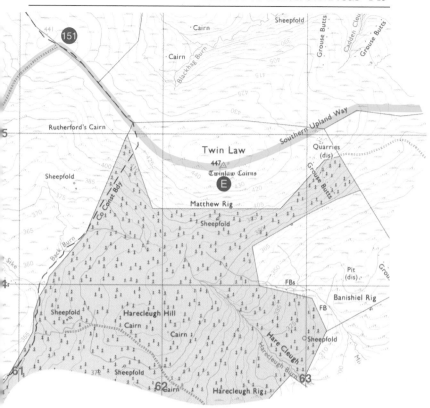

all the way back to
the Eildon Hills. The main landmark
is no more than a blip in the distance, the two cairns of Twin Law. The
track heads steadily uphill, gradually turning towards the distant cairns
until it reaches the top of the ridge where it comes to a halt **151**. Turn
right onto the narrower footpath to head directly to the cairns. Now it is
possible to see the end of the moor, the reappearance of farmland and
the glint of Watch Water Reservoir.

Twin Law cairns **E** are extraordinary structures: two round, hollow
towers, beautifully constructed in stone, which could easily be mis-
taken for ancient fortifications. There is a legend that two champions,
one representing the Scots the other the Saxons, fought a battle to
the death, not knowing they were brothers separated at birth. No legend, however, is needed to enjoy this situation, and on a cold windy
day the little niche in one tower is a cosy spot to snuggle into and
enjoy the view, one of the last, and best, panoramas of the whole
Way. It is even possible on a good day to see the sea to the east.

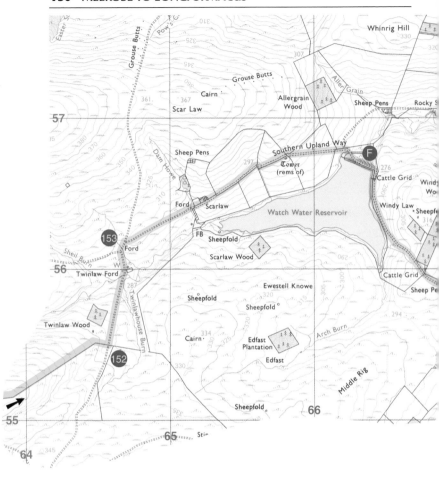

After a rest and a pause to take in the view, it is time to head downhill again towards the reservoir. The path crosses a stone wall and continues on alongside the fence. At the foot of the hill **152** turn left onto a grassy track that soon begins to dip quite steeply downhill to a little valley, to cross a fast-flowing hill stream at the bottom and then climb again up the opposite bank. Then, where the track divides **153**, turn off to the right. The reservoir, which had temporarily disappeared, now comes back into view. This is still pleasant walking on a grassy track through the heather, but as if to confirm that the moorland walk really is over it turns onto a metalled road running above the reservoir, separated from the water by neat, square fields.

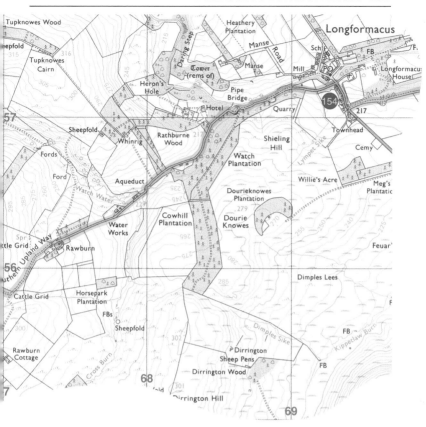

Eventually, the road swings round to cross the overspill channel and cross the top of the dam **F**. It begins to climb again and offers a chance to look back at the twin cairns, and then heads back down for the final walk into Longformacus. It passes the square, rather stolid waterworks buildings and crosses a stream to enter an attractive little wooded valley. Beyond the grounds of Rathbone House, once a hotel, is a pretty little footbridge over waterfalls and here the road begins to run alongside the wider river, Dye Water. The river offers fascinating contrasts between dark slow moody reaches and sudden bursts of sparkling white water as it dashes over rocks. It arrives at a high-arched bridge in the centre of Longformacus. The village of traditional stone houses clusters round the road junction **154** and here the route turns right for the very last section of the Way.

11 LONGFORMACUS TO COCKBURNSPATH

via Abbey St Bathans   *18 miles (29 km)*

The section starts on the road out of Longformacus, then turns left at the end of the houses onto the Whitchester road **155**. This is a pleasant country lane that runs beside the parkland of Longformacus House, which rings with the harsh cries of peacocks. The parkland ends and quietness returns and there is open countryside to enjoy – and a large population of rabbits seem to be doing just that. There are glimpses of the river through the trees as it sets out on extravagant meanders. Where the trees thin out and the road turns sharply left **156**, turn right over a stile onto the path by the little stream. There is now a steady uphill climb alongside the fence, and soon it is possible to look back and see the full splendour of the house and its park. Nearing the top of the hill **157** cross the stile and turn away from the fence onto the clear path threading its way through the coarse tussocks. This gives way to a green path, still heading in the same direction and waymarked by a line of posts until the next landmark, a small clump of trees, comes into sight. A path of reddish clay now heads off through a rough landscape of heather, rough grass and inky pools. The walk runs along the side of the small copse and then continues

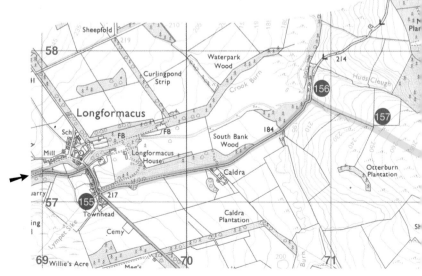

beside the larger patch of woodland, a comfortable grassy track under the spreading branches of beech trees. At the break in the trees, cross the stile on the left and go through a zigzag of stiles to continue on the Way, but now on the opposite side of the line of beech. This is all very pleasant walking, with views back over the heather moorland.

At the end of the section, where the woodland turns left **158**, turn right to cross through the trees again and continue on the farm track that heads past a clump of trees, all that remain of an area of felled woodland. When finally clear of the trees, the area up ahead is revealed as a gentle swell of farmland. The track begins to head steadily downhill, leaving the rough moorland grass behind. At the road **159**, turn left by the attractive lodge with a little oriel window, and then almost immediately right, just before the plantation, to take

the track that winds uphill. Having almost reached the top it slips very slightly downhill again round the shoulder of the hill, a little below the rougher ground spattered with heather and gorse.

Just before the fence at the edge of a new conifer plantation, the path swirls round the head of a little valley and crosses the stile by the gate. Follow it round slightly uphill along the fence to a point just before the deep dip **160** down towards the heather, then turn left to head for the edge of the woodland. The Way goes very steeply down, with the aid of wooden steps, to the little valley and the rather romantically named burn, Robber's Cleugh: the imaginative could easily see this as a good place to hide stolen cattle.

At the bottom cross into the trees and turn right onto the forest road, which now stays on a level above Whiteadder Water. There are occasional glimpses of the river and the fields beyond it, but there is really not much of a view until the trees begin to thin out, and then the road slips downhill to join the river bank for a while. It gradually turns away again, but one can still look down on the bustling waters and the bridge at Abbey St Bathans soon comes into view.

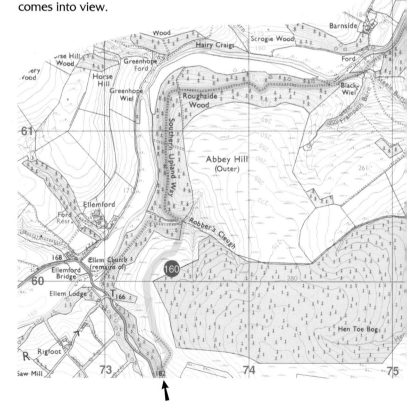

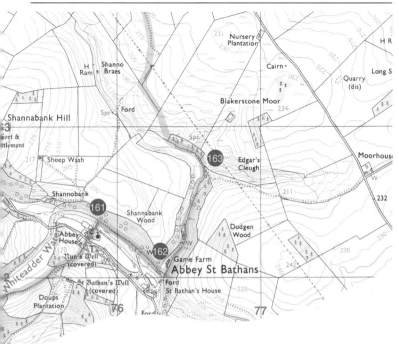

The path comes down past the youth hostel and the church. The church itself, apart from an attractive stumpy spire, is quite plain, though there are remnants of the older priory on the west face. It is worth looking for some fine carved inscriptions, including a notable example of 18th-century lettering on a tombstone in the porch.

Cross over the footbridge **161** and turn right to take the riverside path through the trees. This is a complete contrast to the earlier forest walk – a wandering footpath replaces the broad track; oak not spruce dominates, and the river is never far away. At the clearing by the farm **162** cross over the footbridge and turn left. Anyone wanting refreshments can turn right over the river bridge above the weir to reach a pleasant cafe. The main route, however, goes up the road, where the name 'Cockburnspath' appears encouragingly on the signpost. The metalled road soon gives way to a rougher track that comes up to an ornate cottage and an equally exotic bird population, including peacocks. Soon the path leads out into a delightful little wooded valley, following the line of a gently trickling stream. Where the path divides **163** turn left and now, if anything, the scene becomes even more attractive, dotted with tall pine and splashes of gorse. The path follows the edge of the woods, after which a stile leads into the fields.

Join the farm track and turn left on to the path between the wall and the fence, then turn right to head under the power lines towards the strip of woodland. The most obvious landmark is the little cairn with a weather vane on top **A**, built in 1948 to celebrate the fact that the land had been in the same family for 100 years. There is a bench by the cairn, tempting passers-by to pause and enjoy a vista of rolling countryside. Continue on, passing through the trees to the cluster of buildings by the road.

Cross over the road **164** where, rather surprisingly, there are not one but two telephone boxes. Go straight on up the driveway to what turns out to be the Vauxhall Off Road Training Centre, and turn off on the stile to the left to pass round the buildings to rejoin the main track on the other side of the farmyard. After going through a strip of woodland, the main track turns left **165** but the Way goes across a stile and then turns right to follow the line of the fence all the way down to the road. At the road **166** turn left and then, at the end of the L-shaped block of woodland, turn right onto the farm track with its fringe of broad-leaved trees. There is a real sense of change, of entering richer agricultural land, with fields of grain joining the more familiar pasture.

The Way leaves Abbey St Bathans via an attractive valley of mixed woodland, but soon heads out into open country.

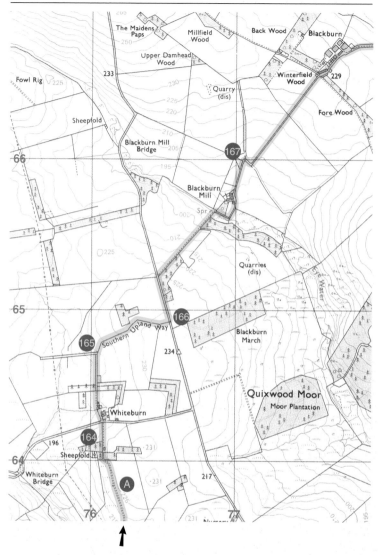

The track swings round to cross a stream lined with silver birch and willow and heads past the house. Now the track becomes more of a country lane, with well-tended beech hedges. Where the track divides **167**, follow the metalled road then turn right and immediately left towards a row of cottages. The change in the nature of the farmland is echoed by a change in the wildlife, as butterflies, notably Red Admirals, put in an appearance. The Way will now be staying on the road all the way to the A1. Beyond the cottages it heads downhill past an avenue of trees, and a deep woodland valley comes into view on the left. The road stays on the rim of the valley all the way until it reaches the main road **168**.

Turn left at the A1 and cross over where the crash barrier ends. At the far side take the path that threads its way through the gorse towards the railway before coming out onto a section of the old road left behind by realignment and now serving as a somewhat unsavoury rubbish dump. Eventually **169**, the old road turns right to cross the tracks of the main London–Edinburgh railway and continues on an altogether more pleasant path through mixed woodland with a little stream in the valley floor. Where the path divides **170**, turn left past the cottage. Visually, this is a delight, with bramble, gorse and woodland flowers spread out among the trees, and only the relentless rumble of traffic to disturb the peace. The path climbs up the valley side through a corridor of gorse and whin, and then, as a second track comes in on the right **171**, doubles right back to head uphill and then

The footpath through mainly oak woodland that borders Whiteadder Water near Abbey St Bathans.

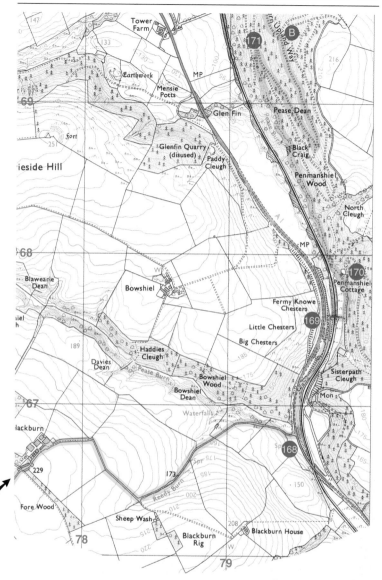

doubles back again to climb to the very top of the valley on an elongated zigzag. Once at the rim, the path continues as a gentler climb until, at the top of the hill **B**, the coast finally appears in view, signalling that the end of the walk is not far away. There is a pleasant sense of symmetry in that shapely Bass Rock away in the distance is very similar to Ailsa Craig over 200 miles away.

Now the path begins to head steeply downhill, and then turns off towards the road bridge **C** that soon comes into view. This is a particularly fine example of 18th-century engineering, rising over a hundred feet above the steep-sided burn. To reduce the weight carried on the tall piers, holes have been left in the spandrils of the arches. In 1783, when the bridge was built, this was still a very new idea. At the road, turn right, then immediately left onto the path that leads into the Pease Dean nature reserve. This whole area is being gradually replanted with native trees, and already conservation policy is having its reward in a notably richer mixture of wild flowers. The path skirts the valley edge before plunging down to the sea on a series of wooden steps. It has to be said that the arrival is something of an anticlimax: instead of the picturesque harbour of the west coast, there is a sprawling caravan park. Wisely, the route planners have not ended the Way here, and the east coast's reputation is soon redeemed.

Just before the entrance to the park **172** cross the footbridge and turn right on the path by the stream for a stiff little climb up the wooden steps and then turn left to join the road. Now one begins to appreciate the majestic cliffs of sandstone, piled up in broad, red layers. Just before the house at the top of the hill **173**, turn right to follow the path beside the stream with its dashing falls, cross over it and carry on up the flight of wooden steps to the coastal path. Where the whole view is opened up, it is possible to see just how fine this coast can be, the tall cliffs thrusting ribs out to sea, with little sandy coves in between. The path turns left to follow the cliff edge, and red sandstone gives way to grey, and a wonderful surprise appears. The east coast has matched the west after all, for here tucked away behind cliffs and rocky pinnacles is neat little Cove Harbour **D** with two piers like the jaws of a pair of pincers. An odd little tunnel pierces the headland to give access to the bay.

Where the path reaches the houses **174**, turn away from the coast onto the farm track, and follow it down to the road. Cross over and follow the track round behind the houses. The path curls round under the railway and the recently realigned A1, and heads off towards Cockburnspath. The official end is still not quite in sight. Turn right at the war memorial **175** for the market square and the cross topped by a thistle, and this really does mark the end of a long, sometimes demanding, but very rewarding walk. And those who have completed the journey can retrace their steps a few feet to treat themselves to a more tangible reward at the local inn.

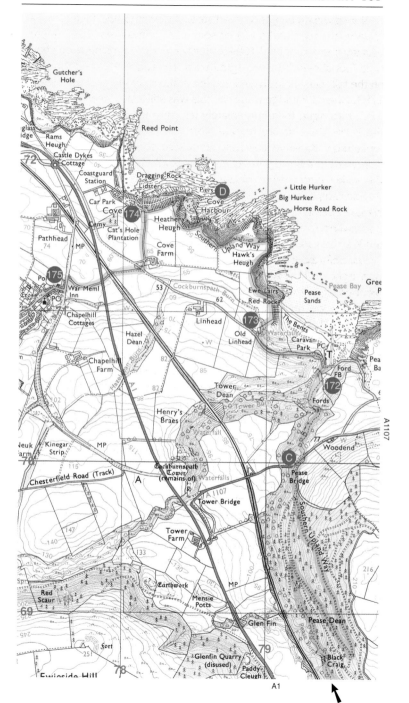

Gutcher's Hole

Reed Point

glass idge

Rams Heugh

Castle Dykes Cottage

72

Coastguard Station

Car Park

Cove

Pathhead 74

Camy

Cat's Hole Plantation

MP

Dragging Rock

Lidsters

Piers

D

Cove Harbour

Heathery Heugh

Cove Farm

Little Hurker

Big Hurker

Horse Road Rock

Southern

Upland Way

Hawk's Heugh

Po

175

War Meml Inn

Cross

PO

Chapelhill Cottages

Hazel Dean

Chapelhill Farm

53

Cockburnspath Burn

62

Linhead

Old Linhead

Ewe Lairs

Red Rock

The Berts

Waterfalls

Pease Sands

Pease Bay

Gree P

Caravan Park

T

PC

173

Tower Dean

Henry's Braes

Neuk arm

Kinegar Strip

MP

76

Chesterfield Road (Track)

A

115

Cockburnspath Tower (remains of)

Waterfalls

A 1107

Tower Bridge

Tower Farm

147

140

130

133

Red Scaur

69

Earthwork

Mensie Potts

Glen Fin

Fort

78

25

Glenfin Quarry (disused)

79

Paddy Cleugh

Ewieside Hill

Ford FB

172

Fords

77

Woodend

C

Pease Bridge

Southern Upland Way

216

210

Pease Dean

Black Craig

A1

A1107

Pea Ba

Cove Harbour forms a fitting climax to the Way. From here it is only a few minutes' walk to the end at Cockburnspath.

USEFUL
INFORMATION

Transport

Information on transport can be obtained from Tourist Information Centres in Scotland. The following centres will also be able to give specific information on timetables. **Rail Enquiries:** Scotrail Glasgow (tel. 0141 204 2844). **Coach and Bus Enquiries:** Scottish Citylink Coaches (tel. 0141 332 9191). Annual bus timetables are available from: Dumfries and Galloway Council Public Transport Unit (tel. 01345 090510); and Scottish Borders Council Public Transport Unit (tel. 01835 23301 X 253).

Getting to the start of the walk
Portpatrick can be reached by bus from Stranraer. You can travel to Stranraer: by train from Glasgow, via Ayr; by bus from Dumfries, Girvan or London; by ferry from Larne.

At the end of the walk
At Cockburnspath it is possible to get a bus to Dunbar, Edinburgh and Berwick upon Tweed, all of which are on the main railway line from Edinburgh to Newcastle-upon-Tyne.

A guide to public transport services across the walk is available from: The Director of Roads and Transportation, Borders Regional Council HQ, Newtown St Boswells TD6 SA (tel. 01835 82330).

Accommodation

A leaflet published annually *The Southern Upland Way Accommodation List* is available at Tourist Information Centres and gives advice on hotels, bed and breakfast and guest houses, camping facilities, bunkhouses and bothies. Companies that organize holidays, move luggage and arrange transport and accommodation are also listed. *Southern Upland Wayfarer* is a free sheet produced by Famedram Publishers Ltd and is also available from Tourist Information Centres. It gives useful information on accommodation and restaurants. Accommodation information is provided in Stilwell's *National Trail Companion* published annually.

Youth Hostels
There are youth hostels on and some distance from the Way. Further information on these can be obtained from the Scottish Youth Hostels Association.

Minnigaff   GR 411663   (tel. 01671 402211)
14 km off Way

Kendoon 2.5 km off Way	GR 616883	–
Wanlockhead on Way	GR 874131	(tel. 01659 74252)
Broadmeadows 1.5 km off Way	GR 417303	(tel. 01750 76262)
Melrose 1 km off Way	GR 550340	(tel. 01896 822521)
Abbey St Bathans on Way	GR 758624	(tel. 01361 840245)
Coldingham 14 km off Way	GR 915664	(tel. 01890 771298)

There are **bothies** at:

The Beehive	GR 221715	near Laggangarn
White Laggan	GR 466775	south of Loch Dee
Manquhill	GR 671945	north of Dalry
Chalk Memorial	GR 686019	Head of Water of Ken, near Polskeoch
Brattleburn	GR 016069	east of Daer Reservoir
Over Phawhope	GR 182082	north-east of Ettrick Head

Bunkhouse accommodation is available at Gordon House Hotel, Yarrow Valley (tel. 01750 82222 or 82232).

TOURIST INFORMATION CENTRES

Dumfries and Galloway Tourist Board, Campbell House, Bankend Road, Dumfries DG1 4ZD (tel. 01387 250434)
Scottish Borders Tourist Board, 70 High Street, Selkirk, TD7 4DD (tel. 01750 20555)
Scottish Tourist Board, 23 Ravelston Terrace, Edinburgh, EH4 3EU (tel. 0131 332 2433)

Open in summer only
Galashiels Tourist Information Centre, 3 St John's Street, Galashiels, TD1 3JX (tel. 01896 755551)
Melrose Tourist Information Centre, Abbey House, Abbey Street, Melrose, TD6 9LG (tel. 01896 822555)
Moffat Tourist Information Centre, Churchgate, Moffat, DG10 9EG (tel. 01683 20620)
Sanquhar Tourist Information Centre, Tolbooth, High Street, Sanquhar, DG4 6DJ (tel. 01659 50185)
Stranraer Tourist Information Centre, Harbour Street, Stranraer, DG9 (tel. 01776 702595)

Useful Addresses

British Trust for Ornithology, Beech Grove, Tring, Herts, HP12 5NR.
Forest Enterprise: 231 Corstorphine Rd, Edinburgh, EH12 7AP
(tel. 0131 334 0303)
Historic Scotland, 20 Brandon Street, Edinburgh, EH3 5RA (tel.
0131 244 3101)
Long Distance Walkers Association, Brian Smith, 10 Temple Park
Close, Leeds, LS15 0JJ (tel. 0113 264 2205)
Make Tracks Walking Holidays, 26 Canaan Lane, Edinburgh, EH10
4SY (tel. 0131 447 9847)
National Trust for Scotland, 5 Charlotte Square, Edinburgh, EH2
4DU (tel. 0131 226 5922)
Ordnance Survey, Romsey Road, Maybush, Southampton, SO16 4GU
Ramblers Association (Scotland), 23 Crusader House, Haig
Business Park, Markinch, Fife, KY7 6AQ (tel. 01592 611177)
**Royal Society for the Protection of Birds and The Scottish
Wildlife Trust**, Cramond House, Kirk Cramond, Cramond Glebe
Road, Edinburgh, EH4 6NS
Scottish Natural Heritage, Battleby, Redgorton, Perth, PH1 3EW
(tel. 01738 627921)
Scottish Youth Hostels Association, 7 Glebe Crescent, Stirling, FK8
2JA (tel. 01786 451181)

Southern Upland Way Countryside Rangers

Countryside Rangers and Wardens operate along the Way. They are
available for advice and information to walkers planning to do the route,
or while on the Way. They can be contacted at the following addresses:
Dumfries and Galloway Ranger Service, Portpatrick to Moffat Area
Senior Ranger, Physical Planning Department, Council Offices,
English Street, Dumfries, DG1 2DD (tel. 01387 261234)
**Borders Regional Council Ranger Service, Moffat Area to
Cockburnspath**
Senior Ranger, Harestanes Countryside Visitor Centre by Ancrum,
Jedburgh, TD8 6UQ (tel. 01835 830281)

Information shelters are located at Portpatrick, Castle Kennedy, New
Luce, Bargrennan, Caldons (Loch Trool), St John's Town of Dalry,
Sanquhar, Wanlockhead, Beattock and Pease Dean.

ORDNANCE SURVEY MAPS COVERING THE SOUTHERN UPLAND WAY

Landranger Maps
(scale 1: 50 000)
67, 73, 76, 77, 78, 79, 82

Pathfinder Maps
(scale 1:25 000)
537 Portpatrick and Kirkcolm
551 Luce Sands
538 Stranraer and New Luce
539 Kirkcowan and the Three Lochs
526 Glentrool Village & Bargrennan
527 Clatteringshaws
515 Rhinns of Kells
516 St John's Town of Dalry
504 Water of Ken
493 Sanquhar
481 New Cumnock & Kirkconnel

482 Leadhills
494 Mennock & Durisdeer
495 Moffat
484 Ettrick
472 Yarrow & St Mary's Loch
460 Innerleithen
461 Galashiels & Melrose
449 Stow & Lauder
435 Oxton
436 Duns & Longformacus
422 Abbey St Bathans
409 Dunbar

Travelmaster 4
(1: 250 000)
Central Scotland &
Northumberland

BIBLIOGRAPHY

Richard Feachem, *Guide to Prehistoric Scotland*, Batsford, 1977.
A. R. B. Haldane, *The Drove Roads of Scotland*, Edinburgh University Press, 1971.
Geoffrey D. Hay and Geoffrey P. Stell, *Monuments of Industry*, The Royal Commission on the Historical Monuments of Scotland, 1986.
Fitzroy Maclean, *Scotland*, Thames & Hudson, 1993.
R. N. Millman, *The Making of the Scottish Landscape*, Batsford, 1975.
Valerie Thom, *Birds in Scotland*, Poyser, 1986.
J. B. Whittow, *Geology & Scenery in Scotland*, Chapman & Hall, 1992.

PLACES TO VISIT ON OR NEAR THE SOUTHERN UPLAND WAY

slightly off route
*Dunskey Castle
*Portpatrick Ecology Exhibition Centre
***Stranraer**
Stranraer Museum, Old Town Hall, George Street
Castle of St John Visitor Centre

*Meadowsweet Herb Garden, Soulseat Loch
Castle Kennedy Gardens

*Glenluce Abbey
*Glenluce Motor Museum
Laggangarn Standing Stones
*Glen Trool Forest Park Visitor Centre
*Bruce's Stone
*Clatteringshaws Forest Wildlife Centre
Sanquhar
Sanquhar Castle
Sanquhar Post Office, Main Street
Tolbooth Museum, High Street
Wanlockhead
Wanlockhead Beam Engine
Museum of Lead Mining
***Leadhills**
Allan Ramsay Library
***Moffat**
Tweedhope Sheep Dogs, Moffat Fisheries, Hammerlands
Moffat Museum, The Neuk, off High Street
Moffat Pottery, 20 High Street

*Craigieburn Woodland Garden
Dryhope Tower
*Traquair House
***Innerleithen**
St Ronan's Wells Interpretative Centre
Robert Smail's Printing Works (NTS), High Street
***Galashiels**
Borders Wool Centre, North Wheatlands Mill
Old Gala House and Christopher Boyd Gallery, Scott Crescent
Peter Anderson of Scotland Cashmere Woollen Mill, Nether
Mill, Huddersfield Street

*Abbotsford House
Melrose
Teddy Melrose, Scotland's Teddy Bear Museum
Melrose Abbey, Main Square
Priorwood Garden (NTS)
Trimontium Exhibition, Ormiston Institute, The Square
Melrose Motor Museum, Annay Road
Eildon Fort

Thirlestane Castle
Abbey St Bathans Trout Farm
*Edin's Hall Broch
Pease Dean (Scottish Wildlife Trust)
*Dunglass Collegiate Church